Raising a Sane
and Successful Teen

By Mary Ann Maggiore

Maggiore Communications

First edition 2014

ISBN: 0692326960
ISBN-13: 978-0692326961

To Gina, Max, Rogelio and Violetta,

who taught me most of what I know.

Table of Contents

Acknowledgements

Helping create a sane and successful teenager is a magnificent process. In the course of seven years, your child changes tremendously, and in that time, you change too.

I wasn't born a good parent; my kids made me a good parent. And there were many others who helped us create a web of good kids, good parents, and good family. It was not always this way in my life; I came from a family very different from the one I created. When I had my children, I decided there were some things about my family I grew up in that I liked—and some things I didn't. I tried to create my own unique family. It worked well. Gradually, I took what I knew and used it to help other kids and other parents, and so the learning grew.

Therapy was a big part of my growing. Karen Johnson of San Francisco and Maxine Libros of Philadelphia helped me more than I can ever say. Teachers, spiritual directors, advisors, physicians and healers all made me year by year a better and better parent. I include among these Charles Hertz, our first pediatrician, Guinevere Maria, Sister Patricia King, Bob Kimball, and Josefina Garcia as some of my greatest guides. There is no parent without a child, and my children Gina and Max have been terrific in every stage teaching me how to be with them, how to understand them, and how to appreciate the children of others. As our family grew, Rogelio brought me vital new learning, and so did our much beloved Violetta.

My work with the young people of Five 4 Five -- my non-profit for at-risk youth -- also gave me much incredible experience and knowledge. Thank you Alberto, Koby, Ricardo, Lily, Ollie, Maura, Kerlin, Sofia, Josue, Vinnie and dozens of others. And thanks to the big people too: To Jeanine Alexander Howley and Peter Howley, Lori Goldwyn for reading and commenting again and again. To Doug Humes, for his amazing friendship and incessant support. To Fay Landau, who is my advisor extraordinaire and to Anne Doyle who designed this book cover, I say a thousand thank yous. To Alison Kennings Massa, brilliant thinker and editor, I am so grateful. You brought the whole thing together.

To everyone, big and small, young and old, who shared their lives with me, thank you for giving me your knowledge, your insights, your wonder and your sense of personal adventure.

Introduction

Like most people I have lived both a common and an uncommon life. I grew up, went to college, married, had a family, got divorced, and carried on—a typical modern American life.

I have been the Mayor of a town in one of the country's richest counties. And I have also lived and worked in South Central Los Angeles among the country's most neglected. I have lived atop a hillside in Tuscany. I have done research in Havana. I have taught Love Letter writing on a cruise ship in the Mediterranean and I have written radio announcements for the Campbell Soup Company. I have been a chaplain visiting the sick and the dying at a hospital. And I have helped children create new and vital lives.

I have raised my own two teenagers. I have taught and guided hundreds of teens in programs and commissions for many years. And through it all, teenagers and what I call "new adults" have remained my favorite people.

Along the way I met, hung out with, and guided hundreds of teenagers and young adults. Some were very poor and some were pretty rich. Some could tell a Crip from a Blood a mile away and some couldn't find Paris on a map. Some had been to Paris. Twice. Or three times. Some had lived in dumpsters for a while; some had lost a parent or both parents. Some had never seen a play. Some had never seen real sickness or death.

But all of them had a singular quality that captured my imagination. They all had ambition -- they all wanted to "make it." They all wanted to capture the brass ring we call "Success."

Call me crazy, but I find the years from 12 through the 20s the most intriguing, exciting, interesting years of a person's life. Sure, I've done the 2:00 a.m. worry-walk a few times. And I have had to appear at vice principals' offices often enough. But I found that, all in all, it wasn't so hard. I had a few basic guidelines and a fair amount of respect, for myself and the kids. And so the rest of it has been kind of easy.

I learned a lot from kids in schools and kids in churches, and neighborhoods and street corners, and coffee shops. I learned from my own kids as well. And what I have learned, I have put down in this book.

Many people have asked my advice or my "tricks" for making this rollicking time in a family's life so enjoyable and so successful. So here are some of the "secrets" I can share with you.

I wrote this book because I like to tell a story. And I like a good conversation. I hope you will enjoy the stories in these pages. And that they will provoke you and your family to good conversations. Children and teens need adults, perhaps now more than ever before to teach them to be strong and focused, gentle and concerned. They need adults to help them learn to find a job, find a love and build a life. That's part of what we're here for. Whether as parents or family members, as teachers or neighbors, somewhere in our lives there is a young person who could use the care and guidance we could so easily offer them.

There is a belief now in our society that the conversation between kids and parents cannot happen because there is a gulf between them. This is not true. The more we listen and pay attention to each other, the more we see that life is still a series of important conversations and a Ferris-wheel of actions. By writing this book I am saying, "Here is my story and the lessons I offer from it. If you like, use it to help shape your life's greatest accomplishment—a happy child who becomes a happy adult."

SECTION 1: LIVING AND GROWING TOGETHER

Chapter 1—My Story

I was born in the 1950s in a part of middle America where adults drank hard liquor, joined the local swim club, and beat their kids. I had two parents who were wonderful in many ways and very disturbed in others. They were Italian immigrants' children and they lived in a neighborhood in New York, which was dominated by the Mafia. They had relatives, close ones, who were engaged in illegal activities. My grandfather on my mother's side was a bookmaker. My great uncles on my father's side were first counterfeiters, then loan sharks, and then longshoremen. There would often be a box of clothes, stolen from some freighter in the harbor, sitting in of my great grandmother's living room. Relatives were welcome to come and take what they needed from the box -- tee-shirts, dresses, dress pants ... . It didn't seem to bother most of my family that we were wearing stolen goods. In our little tribe we were taught to overlook the workings of distant relations who were loving family members to us children but who were also common thieves.

My parents wanted to get away from all of this, and they succeeded. Luckily my father, who had been a handball champ in the old neighborhood, caught the attention of one of the most senior officers on his Navy base in San Diego during the Second World War. The officer had a severe drinking problem. He used to work off his unholy hangovers with punishing games of tennis every morning at dawn. He heard about my father's handball playing and ordered him trained in tennis. Dressed in tennis whites and probably a bit nervous, my father, an Italian-American kid from the streets of Brooklyn, spent a good part of the war helping this admiral work out his guilt over his drinking. My father learned tennis well. He learned a lot of other things, too. He learned how to be in the presence of money and to converse with people who had it. He learned some of the secrets of making it financially in this world. When he left the Navy he was ready to enter a new kind of life.

At a party after the war was over, my father met my mother. Working as a secretary in a publishing house, my mother had ideas of creating a new life as well. The two young people shared the hope of leaving the tugs of the old world behind. So they left the city and bought a house in a very small, very historic town in Northern New Jersey, loaded their two, then three, then four, then five, children into their maroon Mercury and went to what they called "the woods of New Jersey" to live.

It was a fine place to be a kid. It was full of magical hiding places for us kids to be in our own little world. The forest and the river and many paths down the dirt road were all there for us children to explore. It was good to be climbing trees in

"Books were my closest friends. I read alone sitting on a pillow at the foot of my closet hidden under a lamp contraption I had made to give me secret light way past my bedtime."

the spring, and floating in homemade boats on the river in the summer. In the fall we made leaf piles and jumped in them for hours. In the winter we went ice-skating over the frozen river and built forts out of heaps of snow. But it was isolated, and I think for many years my parents were very lonely. There wasn't much activity apart from visiting neighbors on our little horseshoe shaped road. My mother, a young woman in her twenties, spent days stranded in the house without a car, worried about money, lost in forgotten dreams, and overwhelmed by babies. Her parenting methods were the extreme techniques of the harried housewife of her time. She hit us often from the time we were very young. And when my father came home at night, he would often drink heavily and they would fight about money, about work, about their frustrations and disappointments. My father paid special attention to me, his oldest, and often turned to me for companionship. But even those moments -- going somewhere with him or talking as we did some chore together, were rare. Like the rest of the kids I knew, our parents were often people to stay clear of. The less we invaded the struggles of their lives, the better for all of us.

Yet my parents had strong similar philosophies about their obligations to their families. Many weekends of my childhood I remember journeying to relatives' homes in New York where my different grandparents lived. We would often spend weekends with some part of our bold, colorful, and raucous family, separated—as children often were then—from the things of adulthood, and immersed in festivities and music and food. In Brooklyn, we slept three and four in a bed with our cousins. We giggled and listened to the Saturday night laughter of our young parents going out to parties. We launched pillow fights while our grandparents tried, like so many other grandparents up and down that clattering street, to shush us to sleep. There was so much going on in our grandparents' urban neighborhoods. There were candy stores and newspaper stands and fire engines and Good Humor trucks. There were games of jacks and stickball and music of all kinds tumbling out of windows. During the weekend days we spent there, we would go to church and then visit other families or run races down the street. We would climb in the grape arbors in their back yards, shaking the vines so the heavy black grapes would fall into our mouths.

For a while, off and on, I had the better of these two different worlds. I could be both a city child and a country child. But in each place, the responsibilities of being the oldest in my generation were often hard and the punishments for wrongdoing were very stiff. I was expected to assist in many of the chores of child rearing. I was praised for being a "great help" but I didn't have much free time. I was able to take care of the mechanics of watching over and bathing and changing the clothes of infants and babies, but I had only a vague idea of who I was—or even who I wanted to be. I was terrified of discovering myself. I was afraid of life.

Books were my closest friends. I read alone sitting on a pillow at the foot of my closet hidden under a lamp contraption I had made to give me secret light way past my bedtime. The books gave me thoughts, but I had no one to share these thoughts with. My teachers would often lend me books from the back shelves of the tiny classroom library. And so I learned the drawing room manners of Jane Eyre and the intrepid courage of Amelia Earhart. I knew the brain was a complex labyrinth of infinite possibilities, but I had never known anyone who could explain what this phrase really meant. I was becoming a scholar in a school of one.

The pivotal moment of my intellectual life came just as I was about to become a teen. I was in seventh grade. We were each supposed to do a science project in February every year, something most of us dreaded. Though most students concentrated on experiments involving electricity or chemistry, I had recently heard of a doctor who had explored the world of dreams. I decided to do my project on dreams. I wrote down the doctor's name and went to the town library.

The library at that time consisted of two small but lovely rooms with floor to ceiling shelves interspersed throughout, with tall, shining windows overlooking the town park. It was a decent library for a small town of a few thousand and in the course of living there, I believe I read every book it carried. But this was in my beginning years so I still had a 'J' on my card, for Junior reader, meaning I had to stay in the Junior reader section. I was eager to start my science project but I didn't know where to start. I went to the circulation desk to ask for help. The librarian smiled at me.

"I need to find a book by a man named Sigmund Freud," I told her. The librarian's smile lines deepened and gradually turned into a frown.

"I can't let you have such a book! That's for adults, and only adults!" She was drawn up to her full height on her stool. Her words stung. Everyone in the two little rooms looked up. I didn't know what to do. The afternoon light seemed to fade from the room. I turned away embarrassed and went home.

That night my mother asked me about my science project and I told her of my experience in the library. She stood thoughtfully for a moment, and the went back to making dinner. Before I set the table, she said she would meet me at the library the next afternoon. True to her word she was there when I arrived. I didn't know what would happen. I think I imagined that my mother would ask the librarian what she had said and the librarian would explain it to my mother and my mother would explain it to me. It went quite differently.

My mother asked to see the librarian and pulled me near her so that I was standing very straight and tall looking up once again at the woman high on her wooden stool.

"I understand you have refused to let my daughter borrow a book by Freud," my mother said.

"Yes, that's true. We do not feel works of that nature are appropriate for a junior reader. She does not have an adult card."

"I want this child to be able to read any book in this library," my mother said firmly.

"Any book?"

"Any book," my mother said. "Including Freud."

"She would have to have an adult card."

"Then I insist that you give her one."

The librarian was clearly upset, but my mother was very firm. When I had my new card, my mother took me into the stacks to find Sigmund Freud's "Interpretation of Dreams." I left the library with the book and the new library card, which named me as an Adult Reader. I gained a power that day that thrills me whenever I think of it. In one swoop my mother gave me the path to personal learning. I had always been an avid, voracious reader, but in that moment she opened wide the door of my intellect. At that moment she showed me a world that would form me. She gave me the world of books of every kind without censure, without hesitation. Everything I wanted to know, I could know. Deep in my deepest despairs, lost in my greatest wanderings, elated and seeking friendship, wondering and wanting answers, I have always known that I could turn to books.

Even though I was roughly treated, as many children in my community were, even though I was terribly lost and lonely so much of my early life, books helped me steer my way through terrible trouble. Because of books I began to write, and because of writing I was able to think and know myself and know my world. This friendship with books, with knowledge and with the process of knowing myself, became a critical necessity as I grew into parenthood.

I did very well in high school and entered a fine college on a scholarship. My parents were very proud, yet the night before I went away to college my father started an angry fight with me and threw me out of the house. He was upset, I think, because I was leaving. Upset too, probably, that he had wanted to go to college and had been forced by his father to stay home and work for the family business, which soon went bankrupt. He did not say all this to me; I think he did not know himself very well. He lacked easy access to what we might call his "interior world." He only knew that he wanted me out of his sight. So, I walked in the dark the two miles over country roads to a friend's house. I spent most of the night there sad and unnerved. I called my mother to tell her where I was and to ask for a ride home. She was furious that I had shared my family story with anyone.

"Aren't you ashamed of yourself?" she asked and accused me in the same tone. I climbed into the car and sat with her stony silence all the way back to our house. In the morning, I came down to the practicalities of breakfast and packing the car. No one spoke to me. When we drove to my new school, neither one of my parents mentioned the night before. I tried to bring it up. They firmly changed the subject. We traveled, manufacturing cheerful talk, a hundred miles along the highway and into the next state. They left me with heartfelt tears and promises to write. I swallowed my anguish and turned resolutely to my new life, resolving to do my best.

I struggled through college. It wasn't easy for me. I fell in and out of love. I smoked a lot of marijuana. I skipped a lot of classes. Toward the end of my four years there, I met a young man and we began a love affair that led to our living together. I knew my parents would be horrified, so I kept it as a secret from them. After months of pretending, I had a nervous collapse and ended up in the hospital. The surgeons thought I had appendicitis. They operated. But my father suspected the truth. He took my boyfriend out for a drink and asked him, "You're shacking up, aren't you?" My boyfriend said yes and my father became enraged. He went home and wrote me a letter disowning me. The condition for re-entry in the family? I had to marry my boyfriend. My boyfriend was amenable. He wanted to do the right thing. We were married. I was permitted back into the fold.

But my father did not believe I had been chastised enough. He alluded to me as a whore at a large family function. I told him he was wrong to call me that. He told me, "I am your father. I can speak to you any way I like." I was stunned—and miserable. Having complied with every family compunction, I was still to be shamed and shamed again. I did not know what to do.

Then I discovered that I was pregnant. It began to dawn on me that my father would continue to treat me shamefully for the rest of my life, in front of family and in front of my child. I told him I was pregnant and I wrote to him telling him that I could not have him continue to treat me badly. He would have to change his way of relating with me or we could not see each other. He responded by contacting all of our family and ordering everyone to cease all contact with me. Except for my grandmothers, everyone complied. My family, my formative life, disappeared. Done. Gone. I had my baby. No one from my family came to see me—no presents, no letters of congratulations. I cried and I cried and I cried.

I do not know at what point in that muggy city summer of my daughter's birth, between the diapers and the traffic and heat, I came out of my stupor and my horror, at my lonely state of affairs. I remember only waking to the resolution that I had to do something more than keep my baby clean and feel sorry for myself. I sat down and began my plan. Gradually it came to me out of a state of total dejectedness, that there were obvious benefits to being so thoroughly rejected by my family. Now that they were no longer present in my life, I would have to mother this baby without their input or support. How would I do that? I knew from my readings in college biology that every baby grew as a result of both genetics—what they had inherited from their parents—and their environment—how they were treated and what they gained or lost from the world around them. So if a baby was the result of all those things, what could I, as a parent, offer that would create a happy, healthy person? I had heard it said that a parent's job was to create a healthy ego in their child and then help that ego function in the larger world. I decided that if I could do just two things—raise a child to think well of herself, and be able to integrate herself into the world—I would be doing a good job.

I decided not to look to the past of my parents and all the people that had come before me, but to teach myself the present. I had begun to work on this plan without knowing it, even while I was pregnant. I had begun already to be aware of living the pregnancy in conversation with the fetus within my womb. Many people, even comic strips, made fun of women like me who took care of what they ate, what music they listened to, and what they said to the baby in their minds. We all had a good laugh about it. But, many of us parents did persist in taking the gentlest care that our babies would come out strong and healthy into a world that welcomed them, and showed them as much as possible that it was safe to be here. Birthing classes, birthing centers, home births, better baby food, safer baby equipment, and safer clothing and toys, all rose out of an old idea that had become a new one. Babies need to be cared for and when we care for them well, they are healthier, happier, and more fun.

So I planned on the physical level to be a thoughtful, caring mother to Gina, my baby, while she was inside me. When she came out of me, I realized while I didn't know much about what she needed, if I were alert to her, she would tell me. So having been in conversation with a fetus, I now began to live in conversation with Gina, the baby. I discovered that my main task was to be a helpmate to the person developing before me and thus I learned to be a good mother of an infant. Then when she was no longer an infant, I realized I would have to learn to be a mother of a developing baby. This required me to learn some new skills as well as to maintain my old ones. And so it occurred to me that this development on my part was never really going to stop. As Gina developed from infant to baby, to toddler, to child, to pre-teen, to adolescent, to adult, I would also have to develop myself as a parent of a baby and then grow into being the parent of a child, and from there to being the parent of a pre-teen, an adolescent, an adult, in that order. As she grew, I would need to grow, too, and so we both grew. We grew together.

I make it sound so easy, and most of the time it was. The easiest path to good parenting is one we all know. The First Law of Parenting is Love, and love is simply paying attention. When you pay attention you grow to know the baby's cry, the child's fretfulness, the young person's longings, the adolescent's secretiveness, the young adult's springing into freedom, and you can hear those tones and see those needs and elations in every stage. When you pay attention, you know the words that soothe and heal, and the words that can wake a person up to life and give them a boost, or offer them the sweet gift of praise. When you are paying attention to another, you notice your impact, your successes and your faults. You forgive freely and you are often forgiven just as freely.

I was married for 20 years. After Gina came my son Max. But the marriage was a challenging one and it was too challenging for me. When it ended, our children shunted back and forth between households for a while. Eventually each of them came to live permanently with me.

As a new family, the children and I had to develop new rules and new methods -- and so we did.

Sometimes it was tough, very tough. There were times when I was not listening or they were not listening, times when there were power struggles and times when there were disagreements so strong I wondered if we would ever get over them. But this is where the Second Law of Parenting comes in. That law is called Respect. When you respect the feelings and life of another person, you don't shame them, you don't call them names, you don't denigrate what they care about, you don't belittle their accomplishments, and you don't hit them. If you are in conflict, you try to stay focused and calm. If you lose it, you apologize for losing it, and you seek to make amends. By amends, I mean pledging to cease the bad behavior, offering to do something to "make it better," giving proof that your word is good. You pledge, "This is not going to happen again," and you mean it.

In raising a child, you are helping a person create themselves. You want them to be people of conscience, character, and depth. They can become that so much more easily if they see the model of that in you. By being attentive you can tell what their needs are on a physical level—more rest, more fun, more exercise, and better food. You are always careful not to call attention to the attention you are giving. Merely, put before them the possibility of what you are offering. If they accept it, all well and good; if they don't, try not to make a big deal about it. We all dislike the "I told you so" style of self-righteousness. Teenagers are especially sensitive to this. They are trying to form their lives, so they take their independence very seriously and they want to feel they can manage their own lives, even when this is not easy or even when it is not working out for them. If you think there is some aspect of your teenager's life that needs special attention—eating disorders, heavy drug use, failing grades—call their attention to it, ask them what they feel about it and form a plan of action together that will help the young person change to a more positive direction. But be aware that a teenager's changing usually means that it is time for you to change too. Be ready to examine your own life, even as you are calling your teen to examine theirs.

Also be aware that in many cases, when a young person is troubled or in trouble, you will probably need more than your own family resources to help you and your teen work the problem out. Don't be too proud to ask for help.

I don't know all the answers. Who does? But I have raised my kids through the fateful journey of their teen years and into happy adulthoods. And I have helped dozens more over the years since then. What I know from my journeys with them I share with you here.

Chapter 2—The Only Two Rules You'll Ever Need

Let's start with two simple rules. To initiate the rules, you need to begin from a positive point of view—peaceful place, a quiet weekend morning or afternoon will do. Begin with a note of truth, followed by a note of optimism. Something like:

"I'd like to make sure we are always in good communication with each other. You get what you need and I get what I need. So I am going to suggest two rules that I think will work for both of us." Then launch in.

Rule Number One—You must have good manners. This means you must be kind to me and kind to others in the world. Don't become a doormat; but do take care, whether it's at the dinner table or driving a car, that you treat people with respect.

Rule Number Two—As much as it is within your power, you must seek to survive me. Don't do anything so stupid or so dangerous that it might get you killed. Your job is to live long after I do.

These rules are so simple, they are almost laughable. You would think at first that they couldn't be that effective. Yet oddly enough, I have found, over many years of practice, that these rules cover a tremendous amount of ground. And here's why:

Rule Number One

"Be gentle, be kind, be considerate." Though we often forget them, manners are the great civilizing power of our species. Manners are what keep us from punching people when we are angry. Manners steady us when the line at the post office seems so tedious. Manners help us slow down, look before we act, and think before we speak. In those moments where manners lay their claim, compassion often steps in, giving us a chance to not only act more reasonably, but to see more clearly beyond our selves. This "seeing beyond one's self" is one of the most important skills you can help your teen attain.

Every time we say please or thank you to someone, hold a door for them, carry their grocery bag, chew with our mouths closed, or tell them we love them, we are increasing our manners quotient, and also improving our lives and the life of the world around us. Regardless of their personality or their developmental level, this rule helps your teen create their own guidelines for behaving well in the world. And that's so much of what great parenting is all about—that a young person eventually becomes self-motivated and does not need us to remind them of what needs to be done. They can approach a situation on their own and give it what they know it rightfully needs.

"Call me crazy, but I find the years from 12 through the 20s the most intriguing, exciting, interesting years of a person's life."

Kids want to be decent human beings. They like to be treated well. And they can be persuaded, more times than not, to treat others well, too. Even if they don't always follow the rule, or even if they give the impression of not listening, the rule has an inner engine that will, over time, do its work. Be patient. Don't fight over it. Be firm. Step back. Let some time pass. As months and years go by, you may see that the value of this edict takes hold. It can be very powerful.

Rule One gives your teen the guideline he or she needs to rectify many foibles: Forgetting to take out the garbage. Leaving wet laundry in the washing machine. Borrowing clothes without asking. Neglecting to call when they will be late for dinner. When you point out any of these misfortunes, say how you want the situation corrected and leave the conversation without threats or anger. You will be amazed at how often situations rectify themselves.

Rule Number Two

Rule Two, as we have noted, says: "As much as it is within your power, you must seek to survive me." Because the rule states, "As much as it is within your power," it offers your teen the chance to reason with their own faculties. Gradually as your teen grows up, the rule puts them in the driver's seat of their lives. When they are new to the rule, they start by avoiding trying to hurt themselves because you have stipulated it as being for your sake. But ultimately they will see the wisdom of these words and start to make more judicious choices in general.

Rule Two covers a multitude of areas. It can be invoked to warn a teen off a crazy diet, or convince them to quit smoking. It can also help them to see that self-destructive behaviors may hurt others as well as themselves. This will give them an out when there is a crazy bungee-jumping-off-of-bridges escapade being planned. A breezy "My mother made me promise not to die before she does," can show a sense of humor in telling a friend "No." This is the kind of "No" that just might save your kid's life. And other kids' as well.

We don't want to raise kids who cannot take risks, or who are afraid of healthy adventure. We also don't want to raise kids who think we don't care. If they think we don't care, they will do things that they are not ready for, or which will put them in high chances of mortal danger. When your child says, as each of mine has, "I'm going out to this party tonight and I've got a ride home," and you say, "Who's driving?" and they say "Jake." And you say, "Isn't Jake the kid who was kicked out of school for coming drunk to math class?" And your teenager says "Yeah," then you've clearly got a Rule Two situation. You don't want your child in a car with a person who has a drinking problem. So, you invoke Rule Two. And it probably will go like this:

"I'm invoking Rule Two here. Jake is a danger in my book. Find someone else to drive you."

"Geez! Who?"

"I don't know who. Someone else. Then let me know."

[24]

"But I already told Jake I'd ride with him."

"Find someone else."

Firmly expressing your concern and offering an alternative solution will most often get you what you want. If not, bring out the big guns:

"I could always turn up at the party, you know."

Rule Two is like champagne. It's meant to be served up only on special occasions. Using Rule Two to keep your child from joining a sports team or from going shopping with kids you think are dull is not what it was made for. Using it to keep them from sleeping overnight at the home of a friend of a friend of a friend may be useful. You may be in negotiating mode here and that's okay. You're not being a coward. You're reasoning yourself and your teen to a successful outcome. You're heading up a family, not a military unit.

Rule One & Rule Two are so simple and so fair, and in a way, so funny to hear, that teenagers can get them and use them right away. Try them and see. What have you got to lose? They cost nothing. And they work.

Chapter 3—Accentuate the Positive

Like many families, we came to the realization one day that we needed a fresh start. I felt like I was not getting my more positive thoughts across to my kids. And they were acting accordingly. That's when we developed the 80/20 formula. This formula says that in any task, or relating, your optimum balance should be 80% "Yes" and 20% "No." It is a formula you may have been using unconsciously for a long time. If so, then bravo! But if your young person is feeling discouraged and has no vital interests that excite him or her, then it's time to look at your 80/20 balance.

Here's a tale that taught me how to use the 80/20 formula to generate enthusiasm for yard work in my son, Max. When Max was coming into his teen years, I decided one morning that the garden really needed some cleaning up. I proposed it to him, but he was not interested.

"I hate gardening," he declared. Yet, I knew that he had extensive experience gardening at school.

"But you garden every day at school," I reasoned. Bad strategy. Relating a proposed activity to a school activity is a hard sell. And reasoning rarely works to overcome distaste.

"That's because they make us. No gardening. No recess." Hmm, so should I go the mandatory route? No gardening, no visits to friends? No, because then we'll end up in a head-on collision. Try moral persuasion.

"We're a family and the front yard of our family home looks awful. I cannot fix it myself. I need you to help, as part of this family." He looked at me blankly.

"You want me to fix the yard because other people will think we're messy?" Careful, Mom, he's getting his own arguments ready.

"Yessss," I say warily. "That's part of it."

"Sheez, Mom. I thought you told us not to care what other people think. Right?" He's facing away from me, but I imagine a grin lurking somewhere on his face. Ah! He's got me. Or has he?

"Look, I've got everything out there—a shovel, the rake, the gloves, the pick. All you have to do is . . . "

"A pick!?! You have a pick?!?"

"Yes, of course . . . "

"You didn't mention a pick!" Suddenly, he was up off the couch, out the door and into the garden. The pick, with all its manly connotations of both power and destruction, was exactly what he needed. He worked fiendishly for hours clearing weeds, turning over earth. I followed behind, gathering dead leavings and soon the garden was clear. He wasn't so interested in planting new bulbs. But I could accept that because I got my 80/20 balance and the garden was done.

Max dug 80% of the garden, literally and figuratively, because most of the work involved a tool he really enjoyed. He would even do 20% of what he considered the uninteresting tasks because the pick gave him so much satisfaction a majority of the time.

The 80/20 rule also means that your attitude toward your son or daughter is generally 80% positive and 20% corrective. The vast majority of the time, you think of them as good people and tell them so. When they ask you for something, you try to see that they have it. And you aren't distressed when sometimes a trial effort doesn't work out. My daughter Gina thought she wanted to play piano. We purchased an upright from a neighbor and she took lessons for a while. When it seemed that the piano was not her thing,80% frustration and only 20% success, we sold it to someone else. It was okay. Gina was learning about herself. And we were learning about her, too. She went on to many other things that were much more rewarding for her and in which she both delighted and succeeded instead.

With school you want a strong positive balance, too. As parents, we get better all-around results when we encourage the intellect rather than just grades. Sure, school is important but you are your child's ultimate teacher. Take them to plays, musical events, movies—ones you choose and ones that they choose. Get a membership in a local museum so that you can go inexpensively and often and so they can take friends for free. Keep the visits brief. Don't become a tour guide. You are looking for that 80/20 balance, remember. Half an hour might be just right for a first-time visit to a show or exhibit. Then work up to an hour, then two, in subsequent trips. Watch and learn what intrigues your teen and put more of those kind of adventures in front of them. The same goes for trips to nature. Make them short and sweet and grow their interest and their stamina over time.

As far as schoolwork goes, accent the positive. The pressure-cooker of competition for grades is not making our kids smarter, it's making them more fearful—and that can't be good. When you look over your teen's report card, praise the fine work (the 80%) you see represented there. "I notice all those late nights studying for Algebra tests are paying off. Good for you!" Inquire of the 20% that aren't so great in a respectful manner: "Do you need some help on this history work?" Don't make perfection your guide rule.

Studies show that kids who are forced to only seek perfection often drop out or fail to reach their dreams. Studies also show that doing well or pretty well 80% of the time can lead to feelings of self-confidence and a willingness to take risks when the time is right. These are qualities—self-confidence and a touch of daring—that are valuable in every walk of life.

Don't do the work for them but give moral support that helps your kid keep going. If the homework is too much, step in. Help out. Take them to the library and hang out in the magazine section while they work on their research. Not with a "You're wasting my time" attitude but with a cheerfulness that tells your young person "I'm with you." When they seem to be flagging on a project, go over their thoughts or their outlines with them. Not in a punitive, judgmental way, but with an air of respect for their efforts.

My daughter Gina reminded me of times when we turned schoolwork from "The Loneliness of the Long-Distance Runner" into a "Team Sport." Frazzled by school and work commitments, Gina could not face an application for an arts program that she really wanted to get into. The essays put her into a state of anxiety which made her think she wouldn't be accepted. We developed a system. She dictated her thoughts. I wrote them down. We went over the notes. She typed them up. She got into the program.

The 80/20 rule forms teens who can do tasks, ask for help, work together, and be patient. They don't expect everything to constantly go their way. They learn that life can be great but it can also have its tough moments, too. This rule also helps them to gather comrades and teammates and create endeavors outside of your realm. They might choose friends who are varied—some who are brainy, some who are more on the athletic side, some who have creativity as their centerpiece of life. In choosing a social life they might use the 80/20 rule. And in responding to events in life, you might see it, too. After a meal out at your favorite diner they might say: "The food wasn't great but the waitress was a riot. It was fun." They can take any experience and get something out of it.

The best way to teach the 80/20 rule is to live it yourself. Quit the negative self-talk. Give yourself that 80% of positivity you need. Boost yourself and then you will be able to boost your young person, too. Show your kid the positives of your life and let them know how you are facing and over-coming difficulties. Try always to bring your life to an 80/20 balance. Happy parents create happy kids. The happier and more contented you are, the more likely your kid will be contented, too. It's a wonderful gift to give your kid and one that will sustain them the rest of their lives.

Chapter 4—Providing Space and Letting Go

Young people have a strong desire to be both connected and free. The adolescent quandaries of "Who am I? What do I want?" are not easy ones. Their confusions often show in their relating to us. Let us say that we think of adolescence as a period of moving into a new stage of being. Let us also say that this stage entails a powerful experience of separation. We can then see that it begins from the moment a child first crawls or walks, or stands at a window and calls out to passersby. When they leave babyhood, you may see them grow bolder in their fifth and sixth year when they refuse to dress for school, will not pay attention to your word, become restive with familiar activities and begin to seek the outside world—going more happily to others, to school, to reading, to riding a bike, to learning to swim. At nine, many children go through another independent stage and may begin to rapidly expand intellectually, as well as physically and emotionally. There is a sudden jump to know the world and to be a part of it—a sudden jump to maturity. Many young girls become passionately involved with dolls or a younger sibling, imitating our society's roles of mothering and building a family. Boys may be building things, and they also may be tough guys at school, setting out territories, fighting, getting into trouble. Both genders may become suddenly disrespectful to their parents, teachers, and mentors. There is a great stretching here, and then a dropping down into a seriousness you may not have seen before. Your pre-teen may develop a new need for privacy and fantasy. This is the time when kids build forts in their closets and snuggle up on a rainy day with a book. They may take to creating things—a model or an invention of their own particular kind of inventing. They may teach themselves an art or an aspect of science, or they may attain physical skills only hinted at before. Athletics may become a passion, whether with a team or on their own. They may begin to refuse rides to a friend's house. They want to walk there themselves. They may be a little vague about what they did with their day. In other words, you, the parent, no longer know where they are and what they are doing all the time. These are natural signs of future adulthood showing themselves. They are games and vivid explorations not to be treated lightly. As they move into their teen years, new adventures in learning, travel, creativity, and physical activity become more precious to your teen. They are the "real deal" for them and in many cases, this is the base from which many future accomplishments are built.

Your job with a teen is to step in when necessary, and draw back when appropriate. Remember this is the stage where they must gradually leave you and complete their inner selves; "Individuation" is what psychology has been calling it.

Think of some "growing houses" now popular in Scandinavia. The structure of the house is such that parents and babies and very young children live in rooms together or very close to each other. The house also contains slightly more remote rooms, so as children mature they live further and further away from their parents. In teen years, there is a room with its own entryway where the teen lives until she or he is ready to launch. Teens practice coming and going more and more independently until they are truly ready. Then they head out on their own.

This stage, this oddly amorphous phase of being in the family but withdrawing from it at the same time, takes some parents and kids two or three years. Some take close to ten. But it is so necessary to see it through, and to judge what is necessary by what you see and know of your young person. How ready are they? Where are their gaps in readiness? How can you help them fill those gaps?

Many parents consider the best first stage is the teens going away to college. But most teens are ready long before that to test boundaries, to stay out all night, or to "forget" to call home. Some scolding is necessary; it is part of the drama of raising a teen. Be aware that scoldings that seem to go nowhere often have a delayed effect. Gina continued to keep a messy room for years into her new adulthood. No amount of suggesting or urging would change her. When she bought a house at the age of 23, she suddenly became very neat and organized and many of the early trial lessons of our living together started to appear.

"I'm an adult now," she told me. "I've got to be able to find stuff."

We started Max on regular household chores when he was nine and he had to be reminded of his chores every day for another nine years. When he moved to NYC at 18, he rented a room first with a woman who was a student, and then another from a woman who was a schoolteacher. In each case the woman held the lease and so each woman established the house rules. They were not going to put up with mess in the bathroom or dirty dishes in the sink. When Max came home at Christmas, we were in the midst of a holiday party. He joined in and when everyone went to bed, Max stayed up to clean up and put all in order.

"Max," I said early in the morning when I awoke to a spotless house. "I don't mean to complain but you were never a neatnick. What changed you so?"

Max smiled "I've spent most of this last year sharing apartments with women. And women don't take your shit."

'Nuff said!

A watchful eye as this process of connecting and letting go evolves is, of course, essential. Do be on the lookout for crazy habits, like your kid coming home drunk or stoned, or complaints from others warning you something is wrong. Invoke either one or both of the Two Basic Rules. Most kids do stupid things and many get in trouble. Guide them through it and out of it—judiciously and firmly. But unless it is a desperate situation, be aware that most of the time they are "misbehaving" because they are making a new path to a new life and there will be mistakes and mishaps along the way.

Do try to stay out of their rooms and away from their diaries. Their thoughts and feelings are their own; they don't belong to you.

Chapter 5—When Nothing Works

At one point shortly after I left my marriage, I had little money to set up a new household. Boats in our area were easy to come by for not too much money. I purchased an old boat from a charitable organization and found a slip on an ancient dock on the bay. There we spent a long year, which included two winters, while I gathered myself after leaving a long marriage and attempted to raise my sixteen year-old daughter and my seven year-old son. Our home on the water was a long-standing boating and artist community that was struggling for funds to refurbish itself. Our boat was old and struggling, too. There were no amenities in this world that swayed between land and water. We shared public bathrooms, and a laundry room with 30 other households, The docks were rotted, so electric connections were too weak to support lamps or electric heaters. We slept and ate and studied in our unheated 35-foot scow. If you imagine walking 300 feet to the nearest bathroom in pouring rain, arriving at a locked door to wait for ten minutes while your neighbor finishes, then you have some idea of what those months were like. As the teenager and resident girl, Gina had the forward v-berth of our boat so she would have a modicum of privacy. Max and I shared the open space of the rest of the cabin dining room, galley, kitchen, and sleeping area all rolled into one. It was a 200 square-foot interior space, which is not much for any family. It was tough. We took over the boat the first week of February and it rained and froze practically every day that season. We were adjusting to being a family without a dad in our home, as well as learning to live on a boat. This meant emptying the bilge when the pump would not suck, filling the water tank with water, going without the comfort of heat, walking in all kinds of weather to the shore to join the earth-bound world. In other words, it was a very, very hard time of adjustment.

Gina was 16 and needed a lot of attention. And she deserved it. The stresses of our situation did not alter the fact that she was a teenager—ambitious, trying to make good grades in a very competitive school, looking for a boyfriend, learning to drive. She was stressed out and so was I. One night all the changes and demands just ran us both into the ground. We had a fight. Gina needed space and time to herself and all she could get was the space her body filled on her bed when she lay down. She started ranting about how stupid the boat was and how she didn't have enough room to stand up in her cramped "bedroom." She felt she wasn't getting any emotional support either. As she lay in her berth shouting up to me standing facing her from the galley above, I could see she was feeling just wretched. I had read the parenting books. I had taken the workshops. I was sure I could manage this interaction.

I kept my cool. I used "I" statements. I kept a smooth and empathic tone. I repeated back to her what I thought she was saying to show her I was actively listening and digesting what she said. I asked her to make suggestions that would make things better. When that didn't work, I made my own suggestions. She could go to the library to get away from her situation for a bit. Or, her brother and I could go to the library so she could have some privacy. I could drive her to visit a friend. Each thing I said seemed to make her angrier and angrier. It all seemed to be going nowhere.

Suddenly Gina became suspicious that I was patronizing her. "You're just standing there like none of this means anything to you!" she screamed—and screamed some more. I really was starting to see red at that point. The quarrel had gone on for a long time and I was weary, hurt, insulted. I had tried to be assertive and calm and solution-oriented. What I was getting was an emotional slap in the face. Suddenly, I had an image of her as a gorilla out of control and coming at me, and me growing so furious and hitting her in the face.

"This means plenty to me," I said tightly.

"Really?" she jeered. I decided to tell her the truth.

"Right now I have an image of great violence against you," I told her. "But I am trying to control myself."

"Violence?" she queried, revving up her anger machine for another stroke. "What kind of violence?"

I was firmly keeping a lid on it as I said, "I have this image of hitting you in the face." I looked at her. Our eyes were locked, but I still had not lost control of my voice or my assertive techniques.

"You mean you are so pissed off at me that you have a picture of hitting me and still you're talking to me like you're all calm and collected?"

"Yes," I said softly, a little proud of myself.

"Fuck you!" Gina screamed at the top of her lungs.

And I laughed. It came suddenly, straight from my belly like a sneeze you don't expect. I laughed. The truth will often make you cry. But it will also often make you laugh. It took a lot of mollifying to prove to Gina that I heard her and that she was right. She deserved a mother, not a therapist. She wanted an argument and she had gotten psycho-babble. I couldn't help her because I was tapped out. But she still needed help and support. So I tapped others beside myself who had the energy and the time for that support.

After Gina and I had calmed down a bit, I told her what we needed were doulas—people who could help her when I couldn't. Doulas, as you probably know, are popular in many other countries, and now in the US too, as support systems for new mothers and their young babies. I figured I needed help with my young teen. We would create Gina's own new doulas —people who could extend the maternal support Gina needed into a big, strong net that could hold her up and give her some bounce, and some place to rest and swing lightly when she needed it. I couldn't give her everything she needed all the time but there were others who could help. I called four friends and told them what was up with me and Gina. I asked if they would be on hand for her when

"Doulas, as you probably know, are popular in many other countries, and now in the US too, as support systems for new mothers and their young babies."

she needed mother love beyond what I could give her. All of them said yes. Gina knew them all very well and they all not only waited for her to call, but would sometimes call in to offer help or to check on her.

With my phone call to each of the doulas, we established the simplest parameters. Gina could go to them at any time, as long as she let me know where she was so I wouldn't worry. Any doula could do anything with Gina that she and the doula agreed would be fun or useful—go for a walk or out to dinner, sit and talk, go to the movies. Gina was to have absolute confidentiality: She would not be expected to tell me what had happened with her doula and the doula was not expected to report to me in any way, unless she and Gina agreed that it was necessary. And the last, and most important, parameter was that both Gina and the doula had perfect freedom to talk about me however they liked. So, if Gina said "My mother is a control freak," and the doula had had experience of me as a control freak, she should feel perfect license to say, "I know just what you mean. Last year we worked on a project together and near the end she made me crazy with how perfect she had to make everything." In this way Gina could truly share her complaints, learn that her mother is not perfect, and get insights on how others deal with tough relational situations that she was just now learning to manage. The system worked really well. One doula hired Gina for a short-term floral arranging job that meant a lot to Gina. Another offered to take her to her driving test. Another phoned her and chatted every once in a while. Still another asked her to tea.

We are all really isolated in our modern cultures. Cars, cell phones, and computers keep us each in our own little pods and make constant moving an essential part of our lives. So we are not in touch with others as we once were. We are alone in the tasks that most require community— raising children. To do these tasks in this kind of isolation can be crazy-making. It was never meant to be this way. Isn't it time we spread the work and the joy among others? Assigning people to your children can be done with a formal set-up, as what I created with the doulas for Gina; but you may also find that simply arranging for helpmates of different sorts to enter the lives of your children as mentors, teachers, or guides can be just as good.

When Max showed a real talent for physics, I arranged for him to spend time with a physics expert who lived nearby. They worked not on school problems, but on ways of expanding Max's knowledge of one of his favorite subjects. With this outsider's help, an interest became

Max's passion. When I saw that Max liked to work with his hands, I found him an after-school program run by a group of male carpenters and a crafts woman. He learned to build things and to be around men who did work with their hands that no adult in our family could do. He spent his afternoons with other kids and other adults doing new things. He even learned to roller blade. He was in that program for many years and still visits with the leaders of that group from time to time when he comes home on holidays.

Doulas and other support people can enlarge your child's experience of the world, and together you can offer your young person a fuller range of adult guidance, support, and solace than you could ever provide on your own. But what about the moments when you are stranded with an angry teen and there is no way of stepping away and letting another step in? In our family we use techniques to aid us in getting our message across without being destructive. I call it The Game.

The Game

So there you are, the two of you, really furious with each other. Doors slamming. Hard words like circling asteroids spinning through the air. You've nearly come to blows.

Maybe you felt like breaking something. You retire to your separate corners afraid that next time you might literally or figuratively come out swinging. This is the moment for The Game.

The Game is a structured interaction that can help two or more people find out what is going on and resolve issues when things go wrong. With two people it can take as little as 45 minutes. But those 45 minutes can move you from a black hole of anger and misunderstanding to compassion and peace for all concerned, including you.

The process goes something like this:

Sit comfortably with both feet on the floor facing each other. Person A makes a query (see below), and person B then answers for 5 minutes. You can use a timer to keep track. While B is speaking, person A agrees to listen respectfully without interrupting . When the timer goes off, person B stops talking. Person A then says "Thank you." Nothing more, just "Thank you."

Take a short break, then reverse the roles. Person B now asks Person A a query and listens for 5 minutes. Do this until each partner has asked and answered three times. Alternate between the three following queries:

- "Tell me something you think we agree on."

- "Tell me something you like about me."
- "Tell me something you think I should know."

After each query, it is important to say "Thank you" to keep in the spirit of The Game and remind each partner to remain in mutual respect of the process.

Here are the rules:
- Speak only from your own experience.
- Don't comment on what has been said before.
- Take a break of a least a few minutes in between each session.
- After the last session is ended, take a break for a few minutes, an hour, or even a whole day, however long seems to work best so the lesson of the words, emotions, and gestures expressed can really sink in.

If you decide to take a lengthy break afterwards before speaking again, try to do something easy in order to stay with the thoughts and emotions you are having and absorb what each of you said. You might go for a walk separately, or one might fold laundry while the other goes out for a walk. During this period, DO NOT DISCUSS WHAT WAS

SAID IN THE SESSION UNTIL YOU BOTH HAVE AGREED
THE BREAK IS OVER.

As you reflect on what has been said, try to key in to
your love for your teen. Try to show the love, not the
judgment, which comes from your intention to heal. Keep in
mind you are both making yourselves vulnerable to each
other. Model the wisdom, compassion and love you want
your teen to attain.

There may be tears; tears are good. There may still be
angry words; these can be useful too. Try to listen for the
undercurrent of your teen's longing and respond to the
longing, not the anger.

What do you hear? - Does your teen feel lost? Offer
reassurance. Does your teen feel isolated? See if they would
like suggestions for paths into community. Are they feeling
overwhelmed? Ask them if they want some guidance. But
don't push. Don't tell them what to do. And don't feel
rejected if it seems they are not interested in your offers.

The body, mind, and soul are undergoing a powerful
exercise of being present for difficult feelings. Just as soup
tastes better the day after the making, human psychological
and spiritual growth often progresses better with some
time, reflection and withdrawal. Take your time.

Be sure to thank them for their willingness to participate in this exploration, and then let go. Go about your day. Things usually get better on their own after the exercise, just from having taken the time to do it. And if they don't improve, try again in a few days. Ice cream often helps.

SECTION 2: PREPARING FOR THE REAL WORLD

Chapter 6— Chores and Work

A child of three should be able to make his or her bed—pulling covers up, patting the pillow into place. No hospital corners, just sheets and blankets off the floor and in some semblance of good order. A person of 13 should be expected to do much more. This is where chores come in.

Chores

First, let me say we need to come up with a new word or phrase for the word "chores." It really has a bad connotation all over the country. Perhaps "household jobs" would be better. Or "family contributions." Whatever you call them, they represent a teen's way of adding to the community we commonly call Family. Ideally, you will have started them working regularly around the house years ago, but if you haven't started them on this simple introduction to family tasks by the teen years, it's time to rev up the training.

Chores say "We're all in this together," and "Your effort means something to me and to all of us." You've been working for your kids for a long time. Gradually kids need to learn how to work for themselves and work for others. Chores are the best way to train your son or daughter to contribute to the household and, ultimately, to the larger community.

Some of the chores that you will train your teen to do are actually chores you did for them. Now you are transferring work you once did for your teen onto the teen. This will often annoy or dismay them so success calls for choosing carefully and teaching them constructively.

Lunch

If your kid hasn't already started making lunch for themselves, show them what a balanced meal is and how to carry it safely and without mess and let them have at it. Check the lunch bag before it leaves the house the first couple of days. Respond positively first:

"Okay, you've got an apple, some carrot sticks. That's good. Now you need a protein—how about some slices of cheese? And you need a carbohydrate. Why don't you take some of those crackers you like."

Then leave them alone. Don't harp. Don't comment. They'll get the idea. You can help the nutrition balance by making sure there's only healthy stuff in the house. This makes it way easier to choose.

Laundry

All teens should do their own laundry; you've done it enough. Teach them how to do it step by step and then make some ground rules about this too. Laundry should go through the cycles, then into the dryer, and then to the teen's room within a few hours. It shouldn't get stuck in the washer for a few days waiting for you to move it into the dryer. Tell your teen that these are the guidelines and then clear out of the way. Get a few laundry baskets so that when you come upon someone else's wash sitting in the washer and you want to do a load, simply put the wet laundry into the waiting basket and go about your business. When your wash is done, you can let your teen know that their wash is waiting for them.

Charting the Practice

Chores that involve the household should have a household chart that you put on the fridge or somewhere equally noticeable. Start with a family meeting—maybe a pizza night to accent the upbeat nature of it. Make a rough list with the family of all chores and determine together which ones are the most complex or time-consuming and weight them—easy chores get one star, hard ones get two. Then discuss with your teen which chores they like and value them with stars on the chart. Then split up the chores so that everyone in the family is doing the same weight of work.

If you let your teen choose the work they like to do, you may be surprised at what they choose. Many teens have no problem walking a younger sibling home from school, but cannot stand sweeping the kitchen floor every night. Some teens like doing dishes, but intensely dislike putting them away. Look for the positive inclinations and capitalize on them. When the chores are sorted and everyone has pretty much the same number of stars in their chore line-up, make the chart and instruct everyone to put a check in the box for that date each time they do a task. Often, you will find that the chart needs to be up for a month or so and then everyone gets in the groove without needing the chart. If there is any severe slippage at some point, re-examine the chart, alter it, and put up the new version. Remember that light daily chores like taking out the garbage may have to be reminded day after day; even, perhaps, for years. It's okay. It is what it is. Just call out the teen's name from the kitchen and say:

"Time to take out the garbage."

Work—Allowance for Work at Home

We live in a capitalist society. People are valued by being paid for their work. Ask anyone who is "out of work" what it feels like. How you introduce your child to work is extremely important. You may have to start the lessons on the value of work with an allowance tied to the completion of chores. The exchange is then clear to the teen. You are saying, "You want allowance, you have to do chores."

Make sure the allowance is one you can actually commit to every week. Sit down first with yourself to analyze all the aspects and determine what you think the allowance should cover and what the weekly figure might be. Tell the teen to do the same. Then meet to discuss the allowance together and agree to what it is expected to cover and what amount is right for both of you. In our household, allowance covered after-school treats, a movie per week—those kinds of things. In any case, weekly allowance should not cover essential food, clothing, haircuts, medical, or dental care. That's still your job. Since our kids used public transportation for school, we purchased the bus passes. But we didn't purchase school lunches. Lunch was to be taken from home. It's healthier and costs a lot less money.

Make sure the allowance is a sufficient amount—you don't want to encourage shop-lifting or illegal activities because your kid is feeling short-changed.

The granting of an allowance is a big moment in a kid's psychological and financial development. How you treat money, how you treat your teen around money, may govern their economic attitudes and abilities for the rest of their lives. If you give the allowance on time and regularly and treat your teen fairly around it, they will come to believe that money and work are happily and dependably related. If you withhold the allowance, forget to pay it, leave them waiting extra days for it, or borrow it back from them, they will come to have an unsteady, unrewarding feeling about money. This can create real problems later in their lives.

One more thing to consider. For granting the allowance, choose a day when it is awarded and give it at the same time so that your young person knows that they can depend upon it, and on you.

Work—Jobs in the Neighborhood

Many people believe that school and chores are enough work for a teen. But introducing a young person to the world of making of their own money can begin on a not-very-strenuous level. Babysitting, doing yard work for a neighbor, car washing, all can be launched as small but successful teen businesses with your help.

Like any growth activity that puts your teen in some new part of the adult world, it is best if you, or someone as good as you, serves as the guide.

You may wonder when you should broach the subject of work with your teen. Oftentimes, they will bring it up inadvertently themselves. The teen may complain that their allowance is not enough. If you think the time is right and there will not be too much strain on their school activities, you can step in and make suggestions.

For the neighborhood-based, small-business task like babysitting or car washing, help them map out a plan; they need to research what the market is

"The granting of an allowance is a big moment in a kid's psychological and financial development. How you treat money, how you treat your teen around money, will frame their economic status for the rest of their lives."

paying. After that, help them make lists of people who might want their services. Advise them on ways to contact their potential clients, and how to create a mini-contract or letter detailing what they do and for how long for each payment. This helps kids do a complete job and not get burned by any confusions about the scope of the work. Be encouraging. Perhaps ask a neighbor to hire them for the first time. Review with your teen afterward how the initial job has gone, and help them tweak the parameters of the work so all parties are ultimately satisfied. At 12, Gina got an offer to meet some friends and their daughter in New Zealand to tour with them as their daughter's companion. If she could get over there, they would cover all her expenses there for three weeks. We didn't have the money for airfare and personal expenditures she might want to make. When I told her, Gina was clear, "I'll make the money for myself." She worked six months as a babysitter after school and on weekends and saved every penny. She left on her own just after her 13th birthday for the trip of a lifetime. She had created her first business and when she came back, the work was still waiting for her. She knew how to work and how to save, and those lessons are guiding her even to this day.

Work—Jobs in the REAL World

This phase is a little trickier than the others. Here your older teen will probably have more ideas and more leads than you. With the Internet such a big part of our interactions, your young person may be using Craigslist or a myriad of other mechanisms to find work for themselves. Help them use research skills to check out if businesses they are considering working for are for real, if they are located where they say they are, and if they are profitable and well-managed.

Help your young person write a simple resume to include eye-catching experiences about their volunteer work at school or in their community, and their own business ventures that might relate to the proposed job. Have them ask a few of your adult friends who know them to vouch for them as references. Don't be afraid to coach them on the job interview. Offer to go with them the first time; you can always wait in a nearby coffee shop while they are interviewed, and then help them debrief afterward. Help them apply for several jobs at once so that they do not get stuck as many teens do—having a great interview and waiting for a call that might not come. That leaves them with no job and no other prospects, either.

When they get the job, be careful to step in with your guidance if there are snares such as responsibilities that over-extend them in some way, or situations that demand too much work for too little pay. Also, help your teen progress with their working relationships. At the nightly dinner table, help them muddle through office politics and culture so that they learn how to respond correctly and professionally to work challenges. Let them know you are proud of them. You should be. They are making their way toward responsible adulthood. Never be afraid to tell them that.

Chapter 7—Teaching Life Skills

Of course the whole time you are raising a child, you are teaching this person life skills by your example. But many skills are best gained through well-thought-out training. In the early years a child must learn basics that they cannot achieve through observation or osmosis. How to ride a bike, how to swim, how to read, how to add, even how to whistle. These are skills we commonly teach our children, or help others to teach them. Teenagers need to learn different, more sophisticated skills: How to drive, fill out an application, manage money.

I tend to work on the principle of the widening circle. I consider any important learning as a series of rings. In the first ring, I am closely guiding the youngster. In the succeeding rings, I am gradually moving away until they can do the task and are on their own.

Functioning in the Practical World

My son noticed one of my methods when I took him to the bank to cash a check he had received for working on someone's boat. I pulled into the bank parking lot, stopped the car and said,

"You go on in. I'll wait here in the car." He nodded and then sauntered off. Suddenly he turned and came back, smiling.

"You're sly," he told me.

"Really?" I said. "What do you mean by sly?"

"Well, the way you have taught me to do things. Like the bank. You start out, you bring me with you a couple of times when you are making a deposit. You tell me what you're doing and have me go up with you to watch you interact with the teller. When I wanted to do something at the bank, you went with me at first and you did all the talking, kind of as my advocate. Then, the next time you and I went to the bank, I did all the talking, but you were right there with me and could say stuff or whatever when it was needed. Now, we go to the bank, you know I can do what I have to do and you'll b

e out here in the car if I need you." He stroked his chin. "Nice work," he approved and left to do his transaction.

This principle of the widening circle, I have found, gives direction and support in small steps and shows the young person the world is there for them, and that the ordinary functions they must perform in it as adults are actually do-able. By transferring knowledge little by little by letting them witness our activities in the world, we help our kids see how we do the tasks. After that, when we transfer knowledge of these tasks in small lessons that involve them, we show them how they may be able to do the tasks on their own.

Banking was one way I taught Max about money. Voting is one of the ways I taught my teens about civic engagement. I'm old-fashioned. I still like to go to the polls to vote. But the steps would be much the same whether I vote at the polling place or through the mail. From the time they were very young, I showed my kids how I research the candidates and issues by going to public meetings to hear the discussions, collecting newspaper articles on the issues, and reading the candidates' own materials. I would tell them what I was thinking about the people and the

> *"By transferring knowledge little by little by letting them witness our activities in the world, we help our kids see how we do the tasks."*

challenges coming up in the election. On Election Day, I would take them to the polling place and explain each of the steps of voting: how I sign in, how I enter the booth and place the ballot, and close myself in for privacy. Then I would have them watch me vote and I tell them what I am doing as I go through the process. The next day, when election results came out, we would review what the results meant and how I felt about them.

By the time they are of voting age, they have a clear idea of what it took and could create their own method of deciding, as well.

Many high schools have courses to help kids learn how to balance a checkbook and how to drive. That is a great idea. But once again, don't leave your parenting responsibilities to the school. Show your child how you keep track of your household checking account. Let them see how much it costs to feed, house, clothe and care for your family. Be sure not to terrorize them with this exercise. Let them know how you started out and how you learned to balance your budgets and make money to do what you needed it to do.

With any skill, you want to constantly increase the level of success. If you are teaching driving, find an area that is quiet and free of distractions for the first few lessons. An empty office building parking lot on a Sunday might be good for the first few lessons. You drive to the lot. Give an overview of what your teenager might be able to do comfortably in the lot, and then switch seats so that your teen can try it out. A good starting lesson conversation might be:

"Let's try circling around here two or three times at 5 miles an hour." Your teen does the circles. You offer praise and then any corrections as needed. Remember to give praise before corrections:

"That was good. You went easily around the turns, and gave it gas just when needed coming out of the turn. When you stop, try to ease into the stop so that you don't jerk so much. Do you know what I mean? Good. Let's try it again."

By making the parameters clear, by treating the young person with dignity, the lesson comes smoothly into their lives and they can interact with the task confidently and easily. None of us is born with the knowledge to function on our own in the world; we all need guidance. We need it whether we get it from our parents, our peers, people at work or from books. A person can learn how to be in the world in many ways. Trial and error is not the swiftest or safest way to learn life skills. The best way is to learn from the guidance of others. And what better teacher is there for your child than you? When we fail to take on the task of guiding our young people, we set them up for embarrassment, low self-esteem and failure. Here's an example that happened in our kitchen one evening:

Functioning in the Social World

I had invited a dear friend of mine and her 14-year-old son to dinner with me and my son, Max. Max was 15 at the time. The young man could not shut up. He talked and talked and talked. When someone besides him started a bit of conversation, he quickly interrupted loudly and recommenced monopolizing the conversation. It was a tedious night for us all. Max said later that he hoped he never had to go through that again.

Another day, the mother and I had lunch together and she said her son was home alone a lot and was thinking of calling Max and getting together with him. Knowing that this was a dead-end street, I told the mother I didn't think this was going to work.

"Why not?" The mother asked me with interest.

"Because your son is very verbal and Max seems to be a bit less of a talker," I said, trying to be as diplomatic as possible.

"You mean he drives people away because he is so obnoxious?" the mother said, annoyed with her child.

I laughed. "Well, that's one way of putting it. He's hard to be around because he talks a lot and it doesn't leave space for other people."

"I know! I know!" said the mother. "Why does he do that? I cannot stand it myself."

"Why don't you do something about it?"

"Like what?"

"Like teach him to be a comfortable guest. Teach him the methods of good conversation."

"But why doesn't he know this already? Can't he figure out that what he's doing isn't working?"

"Maybe he can see that what he is doing isn't working, yes. But he may not know what to do instead. But you're his mother. It's your job to teach him what works."

The mother was amazed, and yet suddenly fully sympathetic to her child, as she should be. Because the mother had given him no guidance in how to behave when asked to dinner, the child could only flail around anxiously.

By coaching the son with positive guidelines, this mother was able to help her son become a better, more comfortable, more considerate guest. Often, guidelines we give kids seem to go in one ear and out the other. But a lot of that "Yeah, yeah, sure, sure," attitude they affect is really only affect. Don't harp on it. Let the lessons gestate. Don't comment. Just mention the guidelines and move on. If you are really energetic and you think it will help, make a list of some rules of good conversation that you've learned. Tape them to the refrigerator or bring them up as topics of conversation at the dinner table. Here are a few rules I learned after years of being a world-class blabber-mouth:

At the dinner table and at most parties, no story or joke should take up more than a few sentences. When you are finished, let others talk.

Don't talk about yourself all the time. Ask people about themselves and what they're up to.

When going to someone's house, bring something to add to the occasion. Food or drink is good. Flowers are lovely. A movie, book, or magazine you'd like to lend can be cool too.

Invite people back. If you go to their house, you're supposed to invite them to yours.

It's easy. And it's fun.

Functioning in Your Private World

All parents would like their young people to clean up their room. This is a cherished ideal. And a waste of time. Teenagers actually need to have messy rooms. They need a lot of stuff around, preferably strewn on the floor, under their bed, and blocking the doorway going in and out of the room. The reason for this is simple. They are building a nest. They are trying to make a cozy, relaxed place to enclose all their anxieties. The bedroom mess gives the young person a place to be, a circle that is snug and protective. It is independent of their parents, and yet comforting. Generally, they collect things during this period. They create these collections because they are reassuring. Collections—of posters, of soda bottles, of shoes or types of nail polish—are all ways of being in a material world in a way they can manage. They cannot afford Ming vases, so they collect t-shirts instead.

With these chaotic rooms, they are also claiming their space as their own. This is a kind of preparation for having a space of their own later when they leave your space. This may not seem to make much sense. But if you have any memory of your own teenage life, you know this is true. It is very possible you also were once a slob or desperately wanted to be one. Now you know that being messy makes it very difficult to find things. Order is efficient. That's why you are orderly. Given the opportunity and the freedom to be disorderly, you might be so. Ask any maid at any hotel; she will tell you that when people have the chance to quit cleaning up after themselves, they take the opportunity with gusto and leave incredibly messy hotel rooms to prove it.

However, most parents of teens find teen mess to be very irritating. Too often parents misinterpret the teenager's chaos. The muddle seems to say to them—"I am a failure as a parent. The one simple chore I was supposed to teach my child, I have failed at. I can't even get them to clean their room." Relax. Give it up. 99% of all American teens are slobs. Yet the vast majority eventually get decent jobs, find mates that care about them, create households that work, and learn to clean up when company is coming. The only difference between a utopian future and the hellish cave at the end of your hallway, is ten short years. By the time your kid is approaching thirty, they will have learned how to organize their lives so their bedroom doesn't emit a smell of dirty laundry every time they open the door.

That being said, I return to a guideline stated earlier— choose your battles carefully. Worrying yourself and nagging your teenager over the shape of their room is a lose-lose battle. There are other struggles on the horizon that are going to make the battle over a disorganized bedroom look like very small potatoes indeed. Let it go. If you are so lucky as to have a housekeeper to help with your cleaning, insist that they ignore your teen's room as well. No use spending extra money on a whirlwind. Twice a year you can help your teen bring some order out of chaos and retrieve the dried apple cores and the old coffee cups and soda cans from under the bed.

This does not mean that your teen can be messy everywhere. Your house is still your house and the other public and private spaces of it belong to you. Your teen needs to help keep that portion of the house in order, even if their room is not. To make household cleaning appealing, in our house we instituted something called the "15-Minute Blitz."

The 15-Minute Blitz

Teens will help with enthusiasm if the chore is quick, intense and fun. That's how we developed the 15-Minute Blitz. It goes like this:

Company's coming! Eeegads! The house is a wreck— newspapers and books are everywhere. Left-over plates from last night's pie are scattered over the coffee table. Shoes, hats, backpacks are piled in a heap near the front door. There are also hockey sticks on the floor, and a can of WD-40 on the windowsill. The afghans on the coach are in a big, lumpy pile. No one should have to face this mess alone. Call the family together, get a couple of shopping bags, and declare the 15-Minute Blitz.

Fifteen fast, furious, crazy minutes that make your living room, kitchen and bathroom look like Martha Stewart lived there. No fighting, no biting, please! Everyone do their part. Throw stuff into shopping bags and cart them to where they belong for later sorting. Fold afghans and lay them seductively along the back of the couch. Stack magazines in a fetching fan on the coffee table. Wipe the crumbs off; put a colorful placemat over that ugly scratch. Move it! We still have the kitchen to do! Do dishes in tag teams—wash, dry, put away. Quick! You only have 6 more minutes before grandma's here! Put at least one clean towel out in the bathroom, give the toilet bowl a swish with cleaner, pull the shower curtain into place, wipe the sink and fixtures down with a wad of toilet paper, and then throw it away. Shut the doors of all the rooms you don't want guests going into. Turn the kettle on, put the casserole in the oven. Now the place is bright, neat, gleaming. It's only taken 15 minutes and even your mother-in-law will be impressed.

Chapter 8—Drinking and Drugs

Alcohol has always scared me. I come from a family of "heavy drinkers," and at first I followed in their foolish footsteps. I can remember a few times in my life where alcohol and I created some ridiculous, and even dangerous, scenes. Alcohol is really dangerous. It is the single most consistent element in teenage accidents, crime sprees, violence, and rape. You don't want your kids messing with alcohol. And of course, they will. And this will worry you. And it should.

Alcohol

We have a very good method for curbing the problem in our household. It's called "setting a good example." I know, I know, it sounds like poppycock to most people, but it has a tremendous effect. You may not be able to control a child's behavior outside your realm, but you can sure influence it. They may not even seem to be heeding it right away. This may mean that you may have an uphill conflict for several years. But ultimately, they will know what is right, and they will do what is right because they know what it looks like.

Setting a good example was not easy for me. I had come, as I have said, from a family that used alcohol to excess. It was not uncommon for a member of our family to drive us home drunk from a family party. I can remember being in a packed station wagon full of kids with an adult male of our family driving down the highway. He was crashing into the median barrier over and over again because he did not have control of his senses and therefore did not have control of his car. But he did have a harrowing control of our lives. It was like riding a roller coaster without the protective lap bar. For two hours I lived in constant fear for my life and for the lives of all those I loved. I still shudder to think I made it through that horrible night.

There were plenty of family quarrels and rifts that I strongly believe were the result of too much drink and not enough self-control. In high school, a boy I knew peeled out onto the highway and lost control of his car and went smashing head-on into a wall of rock. He had been drinking. In the high school our children went to, it became a common Saturday night entertainment to race the strip of highway just before one of the major exits. The kids, loaded with drink, in cars loaded with others who were drunk, were racing each other, eager to win or die. Many died. So many died that the state law for driving as a teenager was radically changed, and now teens must begin with six months of driving with a parent, then six months of driving with an adult person in the car before they can take responsibility of driving on their own. In our county, police carefully watch the time of day, too. Night drivers are pulled over much more easily. And as a result, a lot more kids are spending nights in juvenile hall. No kid needs that. No parent needs it either.

In our house, without being too self-righteous about it, adults try to act sensibly and responsibly. I entertain a lot and try to make sure my guests have the full tea and dessert course before they go out into the night. We have many beds, and guests are always welcome to sleep over. But more to the point there is my personal example that is most expressive. When my daughter was 14, I decided I had best set a clear example.

Gina was new to high school and was of course into trying every social gathering there was. She joined the drama troupe. She helped with the Homecoming float. She tried different clubs, she ran for the track team for a while. And she went to every party she could. Early in her freshman year, at one party in a remote town near the regional high school, she

> *"They say you can break a habit in 30 days. And I am here to prove it."*

witnessed friends of hers getting completely drunk in the first part of the night and then spending the rest of the night vomiting into the bushes outside the dance hall. It was a shock to Gina. She was the Florence Nightingale of the evening, cleaning people up, getting them into cars with safe drivers and seeing that they went on home. She told me about the incident and said she thought it was the amount of alcohol, not drinking per se, that was the problem. I don't believe that 14 year olds should be drinking alcohol at all, and I realized that abstinence in this area was something I needed to require of her. And the best way to require her commitment to such abstaining would be to abstain with her.

I announced the regimen early in the school year, right after the horrendous party at that dance hall. I would make Gina a deal: I would not drink, smoke cigarettes, or indulge in marijuana for one year, if she would do the same. I've never been a cigarette smoker so that was no big deal. And marijuana is not hard for me to stay clear of. But it was the commitment to staying away from alcohol that made it an amazingly tough year for me. I had developed the habit of using one glass a night of Chardonnay to help me through the rigors of preparing the family dinner, then sitting through that dinner with my marriage shattering around me, then cleaning up, helping with homework, and supervising bedtime. The wine made the rigors of the nighttime dinner table squabbles and the organizing of washing up of kids and dishes bearable for me. When I quit the wine—my only indulgence—I really was left to face those "witching hours" without any kind of crutch. For 30 days I missed that white wine stabilizer like a junkie might miss a fix. I thought about it some part of every hour of every day. I substituted juices and teas. I created easier meals. I insisted on help from my spouse. But every day, no matter how I altered the situation around me, at 5 o'clock, I still thought about and craved that wine.

And then I didn't think about it anymore. They say you can break a habit in 30 days. And I am here to prove it. At the end of the month, I no longer craved the wine. I knew my marriage was in trouble. Because I could focus on the parts of my family life that mattered without being addled by the wine, I could help make the dinner hour at least more bearable. My daughter noticed my commitment and claimed her own commitment to her part of the bargain. She stayed sane and sober, and so did I. When the year was up, someone offered me a beer at a celebration and I took only one sip and it nearly knocked me out; the alcohol so overpowered me. I couldn't drink any more. I had a glass of water and an hour later, I drove home.

Since then, I've had a great respect for alcohol and I believe my daughter has too. It is so clearly a depressant, meant to dull the part of your brain that is whirling too fast and maybe a little too unhappily. But it keeps us from doing anything about that whirling, painful part. You cannot focus on your interior life. And when you cannot focus in, you cannot focus outward so well, either. When you are hiding the trouble, the trouble is always with you.

But you are an adult. You know this already. The point of my story is that Gina went through high school alcohol and drug free. She was still hip, all right. Much admired, very popular. So she made it hip to be clear of those things she thought would do her no good. When Gina said, "No, thanks" she meant it. In college she created a female party group that used to walk to local parties and walk back. There's safety in numbers, for sure, so they took good care of each other that way. But they also watched out for each other's party intake, too. It helps when you're young to have someone tell you, "You've had enough, we're taking you home." Eventually you don't need other people to tell you—you know. And that's a big step toward adulthood.

The next thing we do, after teaching abstention, is teaching moderation. When young people are sixteen or so in our house, usually around the Easter feast, we offer them a half glass of some good wine. We might give a few instructions about sipping it, feeling the flavor in our mouths, etc. But in general, it's a special time ushering the young person into the ritual of drink. It is meant to heighten the pleasure of a meal and meant to be taken in small measure. Kids get it.

But in general, unless it is under the most special circumstances, your teen should not be drinking. And you need to be especially careful that their visiting friends don't drink in your home, either. Make your home welcoming without alcohol. Invite kids in and then clear out to another room for a bit, coming in periodically just to poke your head in. Go read a book in the back bedroom or the back yard. Let them know they are free to have their privacy but also give them a sense of yourself as a withdrawn, but still very available, presence. Have games out on the coffee table: Jenga, Scrabble, Monopoly, Backgammon, a deck of cards.

Then make sure there are pretzels or chips and some cold non-alcoholic drinks on hand. Make clear to your teenager that you don't want drinking going on in the house. Explain to them the dangers of drinking and driving. Let them know that you and they are responsible if anyone does drink at your house and then leaves and gets hurt. In many states your household can be named as liable for any accident that happens once your guest leaves the house. You do not need that complication or that guilt.

To make it clear to your teen that you are serious, have a talk with them about it before people start coming over. It is good to renew this talk every year or twice a year until they move out and get their own place. It doesn't have to be much. Simply:

"I know you're going to be having friends over and that's great. There are snacks in the closet and I put some cold drinks in the fridge. I'll be around but out of your way. Just keep in mind I don't want any drinking in the house. I don't want anyone bringing any alcohol in, and I don't want them using any of the stuff that's here. Are we cool?"

The kid of course says yes, because all kids know that this is the best approach in such a situation. They get rid of the conversation and their parent in one fell swoop. If they argue, they realize they will lose, and will create a suspicious atmosphere that will mean the parent is always checking up. They just say yes.

Okay, so now you have been clear about the gathering and the alcohol and your presence. At some point, one of these days or evenings, someone who does not know the rules, or who is there to break the rules, will appear with a bottle of liquor or a six-pack of beer. It is at this point that you must make a scene. Yes, I said a scene. Very low-keyed, so it gets the message across privately to the miscreants, but is so quietly done that it does not end the party. Something like this:

"Max, can I see you for just a sec." Max comes into the kitchen or study or wherever you have chosen.

"Someone brought liquor into this house. I am confiscating the bottles and I want you to inform them and the others that there is no drinking in this house. If I find out there is more liquor here, I'm calling the police. Got it?"

"Got it." Your son or daughter goes out and quietly tells the third party what had been said and warns this party about making their own, larger scene. If they are miffed, the guest can always come to you and in private you can tell him the same thing you just told your teen. It usually works.

Kids want action. If it looks like there is no action here, they will go where there is more action. The movies, another party, bowling, rock climbing, whatever. Don't be surprised if they leave your house an hour or so after they have just arrived. It is in the nature of teenage-hood to prowl. That's fine. Just as long as you haven't abetted the drinking portion of their prowling.

One more thing: The safest protection against your kid not becoming a drunk is for you not to be one, as I have said. The next safest protection is for your kid to be surrounded by friends who are genuine friends—kids who do things, who have interesting lives, who can develop important conversations. Encourage your young person in the search for good friends. When someone stops by, engage them in conversation yourself. Find out what the friend thinks, where they've been, what their family is like. Offer details about yourself and your life that might interest them. Remember they are people and if you show respectful interest in the music they like, the clothes they wear, the movies they see, you can have a real conversation with a real kid yourself. Then, later, be sure to compliment your teen on something good you find in the friend. "Logan's neat, he knows a lot about tea from working in that grocery store." Or "Jessica is so funny, she's such a great mimic, it's amazing."

When a teenager's friend enters your house and you are there, have your teen bring them to you to greet you. By the same token, when the teen leaves, if you wish them to come by again, let them know you have enjoyed their visit and they would be welcome back again. Kids take these final words seriously and they will come back again—even if you don't have booze to offer them.

Drugs—Max's Story

Drugs are a slightly different story, but only slightly. Most kids in high school will experiment with marijuana. As a parent who grew up in the 60s, I had a very laissez-faire attitude toward marijuana. I had been stoned quite often as a teen and so I had a lot of guilt about ordering my son away from it. It wasn't until he came to a family party wrecked that I noticed how upsetting it was relating to a person who was incapacitating a good part of his brain.

I must tell you that Max has always had an enviable mind. A talented actor/director/playwright in high school, he also excelled in mathematics. But he was not meant for the job in the office with the desk near the water cooler. He made this quite clear when he was barely 14. Never one to go along to get along with school leadership, he formed his own path. He took math classes at the local community college. He became the Technical Director as well as the chief actor in his school's excellent theater department. He announced that he would do high school his way. He would take only drama and math; he would read all the history and literature that filled the shelves of our house and at 18 he would take his High School General Education Development Test and go on from there. College? He wasn't interested. He wanted to go straight into the work world. I was nervous, and yet in the areas that he loved, he shone. My son was sure of his path. He was taking it.

At the end of high school, loaded with awards and praise for his work in the theater, Max found out about a program with the California Shakespeare Festival where he would be trained as stage electrician. I helped him get into it and to travel the great distances it took for him to get to this new work. At the end of six months, he took his GED and around that time finished his training with the Festival. He applied for jobs in theaters in San Francisco and got work at The Magic Theater and the ACT and Teatro Zinzanni. He gained a reputation for being capable and knowledgeable. He was also spending his evenings getting drunk and stoned with the 35 and 45-year-old men he worked with.

This terrific, gifted, bright young star was in danger of becoming a wastrel. He was holing up in my garage in a makeshift bed where he would stumble home to pass out. As much as I tried to reason with him and point him in a new direction, I could see it was doing no good. I realized after several mornings of watching him bleary-eyed and unfocused hobble to the john, that my son was in trouble. I had to face him down. We fought for two nights in a row. I said I wanted him to make his way in the world, not ruin himself with drugs and booze and stumble home to sleep naked on a cot. He said he would go live with other buddies in the neighborhood. I tried to explain to him that it was time to find a sober path into the world. He said he was doing fine. He liked his life. I saw him sinking into an abyss. I had never had such terrible nights in all the 18 years of raising him. I was frantic.

I sat myself down in the dark of the last quarrel's sickening aftermath and pondered. This couldn't go on. We were getting nowhere. We were stuck in a whirl of negativity. We needed some positive energy. When faced with the world's giant "No," I always go searching for the "Yes." I wracked my brain. What could change this banging of heads, this litany of disagreeable phrases we were now repeating to each other over and over again? What positive solution was there that would give us both what we wanted? What was something that Max would want more than a dissolute life of smoking dope? It came to me gradually in the night and by morning, I was ready for the summary conversation.

"Max," I said when I sat down at the kitchen table late in the morning. "If you could go anywhere in the world, where would you go?"

"Anywhere?"

"Anywhere."

He thought but a second and then answered me.

"Thailand," he said.

"Good enough," I said. "Pack your bags. You are leaving in a week. I'll purchase you a round trip ticket today. You'll be gone for a month—30 days. You'll pay for your 30 days there out of your own money."

"I'm not ready to go in a week!" he protested.

"You're going," I said.

And so he did. A week later I drove him to San Francisco Airport and said good-bye. He flew away. A month later, after traveling, rock climbing and swimming, he had found a job as a bartender. He lived in a room over the bar. He was still only 18. Two Americans came into the bar while Max was working. The man was in his 30s, the woman was about 50. The terrible Tsunami had happened and they wondered if Max wanted to go with them to a relief camp to build new housing there. Max agreed to go with them. They drove the length of the peninsula to a little village where a thousand people were sleeping in a field on newspapers. There was a team of carpenters from the US, Canada, Italy, and Germany working furiously with the villagers to build new housing. Max had lots of experience building things from his theater work and so he set to the job with a team of older men with alacrity. He loved it. He emailed me that he was staying another month.

At the end of the month, the Western carpenters realized they were close to finishing several of the houses. They asked for a meeting with the chiefs of the village and told them:

"We've finished some houses. How do you want to distribute them?"

The village leaders said, "We will gather everyone in the village tonight and decide together. In the morning we will let you know."

The Westerners went to sleep and the villagers met into the night. In the morning, the chiefs asked to speak to the head of the Western carpenters and this is what they said,

"We have decided that, until everyone has a house, no one will move into a house."

The Westerners were dumb-founded.

"How will we do this?" They asked.

"We will have to work very fast," said the chiefs.

And so they did.

The incident had a profound effect on Max. He wrote me soon after he witnessed this meeting: "I know what I want. I want to be in the theater and the theater is in New York. I am not flying back to San Francisco. I am flying to New York to start my life there."

And that is what he did. At the age of 18, he started a business as a freelance stage electrician in New York City and soon he was working on Broadway shows. He had purpose. He was participating in life instead of escaping it.

This kind of parenting, going for both the positive solution and making a demand that the solution include personal sacrifice and commitment, may look risky. But it is no more risky than spending fruitless years fighting with your kid, attempting to pack their very vital and unusual energy into a mold that does not fit. The answer to drugs is not always therapy. The answer just might be meaningful work.

It still took Max a while to achieve a balance between work and play and alcohol and drugs and his commitments. But he learned. And his learning was his own. By focusing Max on experiences that would enlarge his world, he was able to leave the life of dissolution and enter a life of purpose. And more than drugs, or alcohol, or fooling around, what young people want is purpose. And it is our job, as their parents, their family elders, their neighbors— to guide them to it.

Chapter 9—Sex and Love

Schools have been assigned the job of sex education in our society, but it is not really their job. It is ours. What sex education in schools is all about is the science of reproduction and birth control. This is called biology. What sex education does not cover in its emphasis on mechanics is self-knowledge, personal pleasure, shared pleasure, and relationship. Again, this is not the school's job, it is our job.

Do not mistake me. Sex education is very useful. I know few parents who can pull a condom over a cucumber in a public presentation as skillfully as the school nurse. But most parents are aware that sex education programs are an inappropriate place to learn about the essentials of connecting with other people. Studies show that children are more and more learning their attitudes about sex from the media and their peers. I don't know what your high school or movie and TV watching experience may have been, but I feel certain that these were not good places to learn what sexual intimacy with a real, living, breathing person might be.

We adults have contributed to our own children's mistaken thoughts about sex. We hide our love for each other for fear that our children may be embarrassed by our hugging, kissing, and affection for each other. Most children, even in the sexually vocal 21st century, believe that their parents conceived them and perhaps a sibling or two, and then ceased all sexual involvement with each other. Because we leave sex education to the schools, we do not take the opportunity to instruct our children on methods and steps to connecting with another and creating bonds of mutual pleasure. This makes them anxious and leaves them to the devices of locker room show-offs and pajama party gossips to learn their early lessons about sex.

Like all things with children, it is easier to start the guidance early and build on it little by little. A preschooler will want to know where they came from, and can be shown through teaching picture books and conversations

"Most children, even in the sexually vocal 21st century, believe that their parents conceived them and perhaps a sibling or two, and then ceased all sexual involvement with each other."

how they grew from a seed that mommy and daddy planted in mommy's tummy. Over the years, there are more and more questions, and if you take your time and respect their need for knowledge and reassurance, you can help them see how this whole wonderful thing happens. As they mature to pre-teen age, they may ask you about your sexual history. Be ready for the question and have an answer. Always, always, always be aware that you are profoundly affecting a young person's growth in a very particular and important way. What you say about yourself will strongly influence what they think and say to themselves.

Key among the questions might be "When did you first have sex?" or "What was it like for you the first time?" Be age- appropriate in your answers. Tell them the story of this part of your life in a few short paragraphs that show a bit of what happened, how you felt about it, how you recall and understand it now. This is how, despite my teen's facial gestures and quick interruptions, I told the tale of my first encounter to my teens:

"My first sexual experience was with a boy I loved in high school. We enjoyed kissing each other and I wanted to get as close to him as I could. (Kids' smirks) But I made a bit of a mistake that I ended up having to correct later. (Kids' curious frowns.) I rushed things so I could "get it over with." (Surprised looks—"My mom bowing to peer pressure?!?") There was a big urge among my friends who were trying to "get rid of" their virginity. I felt the burden of it too. So my first time was in a station wagon, tucked behind a school, afraid of being caught by cops; nervous, excited, wanting to do it right. (Kids' nervous looks, perhaps a thoughtful nod of a head.) It hurt a bit and when it was over, I was surprised at how little it affected me. I called a friend and told her, 'I can't believe what all the fuss is about. The Playboy magazines and the talk and more talk about sex. It's like nothing, really." (Kids' laughter) But I learned what the fuss was about later, when we tried again and again. (Eyebrows raised, interested look.)

"Many weeks later, when I was away at college, this same boyfriend came to visit me and stay the weekend. We had our own room and we were not afraid of being interrupted, and we taught each other how to touch and how to kiss, so that it was good for both of us. That is when I had my first orgasm." (Eyes looking down and away. A little smile.)

We know each other through our stories. And these stories can build the character and courage of those who hear us. By telling our stories with grace, loving truth, and a nod to humor, we help our children see a bit of the path we made. In this way they receive a look at our own humanity, which can often reassure them in theirs. We do not ask that they follow our path. And we must mean this sincerely. I cannot say because I had sex at 17, that no one should have sex before 17. I cannot say because I chose a young man, that my daughter should choose a young man or that my son should choose a young woman. I cannot say that love is necessary to the encounter. I cannot say that station wagons are inadequate and beds are better. I can only say what I created in my life and help my teen create something that will work for them in theirs.

Storytelling is very useful. But sometimes instruction is also needed. Check in from time to time. When it is time for their yearly check-up, be sure you have selected a health care professional who will support their health and be respectful of them and their questions, as well. When my daughter was nearing the age when she wanted to be sexually active, she chose to go to Planned Parenthood with a group of friends and not with me. But with each of my children, I asked how they would feel most comfortable getting medical support. So you might offer to make arrangements for your teen's check-up. You might offer to go with them, even if it means that they ask you to sit in the waiting room while they see the doctor alone. Discuss birth control methods and disease prevention with them. Discuss rape and the prevention of rape with both your female teen and your male teen. Don't be afraid to get it all out in the open. Your teen may act like they have "learned it all" in sex ed, but it doesn't hurt to repeat your version of all these important topics with them. You're a caring person and you want them to be healthy and safe.

When you think your young person is ready to become sexually active, decide with them how you can help this part of their lives truly work. In our house a teen is welcome to let the family know that they are having a guest over and need some private time. The rest of the family goes out for the evening and the young person and their guest get the house to themselves for a number of hours. When my daughter fell in love and wanted to make love for the first time in her life, I arranged for her young brother to visit his father for the weekend and I took a room in a nearby hotel. They initiated themselves with dignity and delight and no interruptions, and we all had a very nice couple of days taking a break from home.

Even if you have staunchly avoided any input into your child's sexual history, it is never too late to start gently offering information and insights that will ease the transition into one of life's greatest adventures. Are they getting along comfortably with their partners? Do they feel they are getting what they need from the experience? Again, are they taking proper precautions so they will not get pregnant before they want to and so they do not share any diseases? Do they have any questions or concerns?

Try not to pry or ask for details. These are not your business. As with all things with teenagers, relating your own feelings about yourself or just checking in to see if they are well will give you far more results than judging or summing up on their behalf. "I like the way your friend notices the art in our house. Do they have artists in their family?" will often give you a conversation that will help you both get to know the partner better.

In many cultures, young people are trained from puberty in the ways of attracting and making love to each other. In one African culture, when a love match occurs, males of the tribe take the young man within their circle and the females take the young woman within theirs. The young man is taught how to approach the body of a woman and the woman is taught how to call the body of the man to her. They learn ways to move and touch and kiss. When they are ready, they are left together to make love. I am told many happy unions are made of this method of training. Rather than learn from the boasting of your inexperienced peers as we in our society often do, in this tribe the young learn from the village's skilled craftspeople the art of making love.

[99]

You, too, can teach love skills to your children. Everything from how to choose flowers, what gift to bring when you are invited to dinner, or to how to move so that your lovemaking brings joy to two people.

When my daughter had begun to have sex with her first love, she was much smitten with him. Yet, when I asked her if they were finding joy in each other, she said that she felt it was all going very well until he moved on top of her and entered her. Then they seemed to lose rhythm, and now, after several tries, they were both starting to lose heart.

I told her, "It is very difficult for a man to know at first what movements please a woman. If you get on top of him and move so that it feels good for you, it will probably feel good to him and you will both learn what works." They tried the new maneuver and she reported later that it did, indeed, satisfy both of them and now they were launched.

She said, "It was great. When we were done, he asked me how I had known to do it that way. I told him you had told me and he said 'YOU ASKED YOUR MOTHER?!?'" She laughed. "I said, 'Well, yeah! Who else am I going to ask?'"

Some help is often required. But some is best illustrated by example. Your loving relationship with your child is the first building block to their sexuality. They love most easily if you have loved them well. Your love of yourself, your kindness to the people in your larger life—your partner, your friends, your dear relations, your neighbors—also give an example of how alive you are to life and love. This will help your teen choose people who are alive to them and who are interesting people of depth, consciousness and fun. You cannot guarantee that everything will go well. Just as everyone must have one Roommate from Hell, so also everyone must have at least one Lover from the Dark Side. Your teen may suffer from the agony of such a bad relationship. Try to weather this period as graciously as you can. The late night phone calls, the hysterical scenes, the dramas that go with all bad relationships, will go away so much faster if you just proceed with business as usual, checking in only from time to time. "How are you doing?" will work just fine for openers. A simple "I'm worried. This person seems to be upset all the time and that makes me think you may be drawn into that kind of upset too. Are you all right? Do you need any help?" Listen closely to their answers and try not to argue with them. Signal that you are ready to listen further, when the time arises. "If you need to talk, remember I'm here." Then drop it. Hopefully everyone will come to their senses before too long. If it gets to look too ugly, suggest a vacation away. Your aunt in San Diego would love to see her favorite niece or nephew. And the surfing is great there. Your cousin in Boston or Atlanta could give a whirlwind tour of their city that would change a teenager for a lifetime. Your good friend 50 miles away might need a handy person for a few weeks. Break the cycle for 30 days and you can change any addiction—even the addiction to another person.

Love is great. But even when it begins well it can lead to a down side. Even good relationships can change or fail to change. When that happens, and things start to unravel, it can be really tough on your kid. And on you. Watching your child's anguish is never, ever easy. But with the loss of a love, there is nothing you can do except make plenty of cups of honey tea, offer a shoulder to cry on, and stay out of the way the rest of the time. Don't pry. Don't lurk. Don't take it on too much yourself. The end of love is the end of love—nothing more and certainly nothing less. It is a great sign that your child cared about someone. It means that, if they can do it once, they can do it again. Do not worry, even when the sounds of their sobbing reverberate through the sanctum of your walls. You may shed a tear or two yourself. But do not try to rush the healing. And be careful with your urge to denigrate the lost lover. This can fly back at you at odd moments. This is especially true with a first break up. If the couple splits once, they will often reconvene and split later. If you say nasty words about the former boyfriend or girlfriend during the first split, when they reconvene, there may be a coldness amongst the three of you that will be hard to get over. Keep mum about the lover and offer your support over the long haul. I have always tried to remember that lovers may come and go—but my kids have only one mother.

Chapter 10—Education

You are the first and most important educator of your child. You should never relinquish this rigorous and often-delightful task. Changes are coming rapidly at all of us -- changes in culture, in technology, in economics. With all that is whirling around you and your young person, you need to keep as calm and supportive a course as you possibly can. Your child's mind, body, and spirit depend on it.

The key task of parenting is to make your teen both self-assured and self-reliant. By the time your child enters the teen years, hopefully they have a base of self-assurance. Now, what you need to do is educate them and see that they are educated by others in a way that makes them self-reliant.

Make Your Home a Haven— For Yourself and For Your Kid

Education requires action, thought, and silence. Silence is essential. Make your home a place of peace and quiet and make sure there are times of deep, lovely silence. Night or day, limit, limit, limit cell phone use, especially when your young person is with you. No cell phones at the table. No cell phone or video game use after a prescribed time at night. No cell phone use in the car when you are driving. You are not a chauffeur; you are a beloved family member and car travel means "We're all in this together." No texting to some better or more interesting someone while you two are together. The same goes for games and movies. Limit their use, too. The mind has to rest to grow and it cannot rest while being over-stimulated. If your teen does not comply, record demerits on a piece of paper on the fridge door and when they don't comply a certain specified number of times, take them off their cell phone plan or off your family plan. Sure, it may cost a bit more money, but your child's intellect and social ability are at risk here. You're in charge, so stay in charge with these requirements.

With limited cell phone use, you may notice that your child is more attentive to you and more able to concentrate on complex tasks like studying, reading, learning a craft or conversing with others. They may become more interesting socially and more interested in you, in the family, in the world and in their own lives.

What's Happening to our Schools?

Schools currently are in a quandary. Trying to please everyone, they often please few. Ancient educational methods are in conflict with young people's access to vast quantities of media. These media, as I have said, have their attendant distractions. That is the downside of such high-tech innovations. But these media also offer an enormous range of resources for self-education. I delighted in this new opportunity myself recently. Not long ago, I noticed my algebra skills were so rusty, I was ashamed of myself. Simple calculations had deserted me. I took an Algebra 1 course on the Internet with a brilliant and entertaining teacher who brought me back up to speed. It was fun. It was easy. It was free. I did it on my own time. My son, who had recommended the course, said he did the same thing to improve his Calculus skills in engineering school. Many students I know are clamoring for this same privilege to self-educate. And many schools are hearing and responding with encouragement.

As far as modern education goes, Thomas Paine said it best for me over two hundred years ago: "Every person of intellect becomes his [or her] own teacher." Classroom learning with teachers lecturing, and students sitting at rows of desks, may be excellent for some kids, but more and more we are finding schools are creating small groups of students who meet individually with brilliant teacher specialists. The students then work alone with these small pods of their peers on projects that extend their knowledge of natural science, mathematics, computers, writing, history, politics, and languages—and often accomplish their work with great excitement and terrific speed. Many school systems have developed half-day programs that permit young people to be in class for half the day and work in the afternoons. With many high schools graduating less than 50% of their senior classes, necessity demands that we look at the way we define and frame education in our country as soon as humanly possible.

And why not? The American education system that educated most of us adults was designed in the late 19th and early 20th century to expand the country's school system, to finally reach every child with some kind of uniformity of method and result. The goal was to integrate, socialize, and normalize large numbers of urban, rural, and immigrant youth into our society. For decades, the form of presentation was pretty much the same: a single woman or man commanded the classroom, concentrating on a short list of subjects revolving, hopefully, around the list of seven liberal arts implemented in the medieval period of

European history. This list was in turn based on a form developed as far back as the Greek philosopher Pythagoras in the late 6th century BCE.

Many schools in rural areas offered the most rudimentary education in any case. Students still learned and many of our nation's greatest leaders were taught this way. But many remote schools were not designed to go much beyond the fourth grade. Urban schools were often much better, especially since highly educated young women and men from certain ethnic or religious groups who were denied positions in universities were forced to teach in high schools, and they often did so brilliantly. Both my parents, educated in New York City high schools, were well-versed in history, literature, and mathematics with only high school educations. Their high school teachers were all Jews, many of them with Masters and even Ph.Ds to their credit who had been denied seats on the faculties of the local "finer" colleges.

With the end of the Second World War, the United States became one of two dominant world empires, and things started to change in almost all aspects of society, including education. International political unrest as well as population growth meant upheavals in the system. Fear of Soviet Russia sparked a hunt against liberal strongholds.

The arts and education took a terrible beating as Congress harassed and jailed many of our leaders in these fields. The military budget, enormous during the World War, became even bigger as we committed ourselves to an unending series of smaller wars that were referred to as "incursions" or "police actions." To keep expenditures down, governments large and small looked to capping budgets in "softer" areas. Over the next thirty years, health care, the arts and education were constantly under fire. Labor unions took beating after beating. In the end, while schools burgeoned with waves of new students from our population explosion, and college students were discouraged from becoming teachers. It was considered to be a wasted effort with no dignity in sight. The saying "Those who can, do; those who can't, teach" became the smug axiom of a culture that had moved toward rampant anti-intellectualism.

Still the system kept growing. And leaders, eager to give form to the formless, began to make a specialty of "measurement" and so the swarm of standardized tests was born. Wasting countless hours of both students' and teachers' time, these tests are both hated and generally useless. They do not give a clear idea of some of the key skills necessary to success: teamwork, adaptability, creative thinking, perseverance, or even intellectual depth.

Gradually, the inevitable happened. Students started dropping out of the system like flies. Currently, even those who make it through high school often look back at the experience with horror. In many high schools half the senior class does not graduate. The overwhelming majority of dropouts? Boys. Girls, pressured by an image-based culture, get better grades in high school and succeed better in college, but there is much psychological cost. Over one in four teenage girls in my county have a suicide plan. Many suffer from physical ailments. Their future is not easy. Women in the US still make only between 73 and 78 percent of the wages men make doing the same jobs. With widespread birth control and the pervasive media youth culture, many young men do not want to marry at all or do not want to marry as early as their fathers did. Meanwhile, for young women, the biological clock goes tick, tick, tick. The future looks grim. What can we do? Plenty. Looking to the future, there will need to be many systemic and cultural changes -- the subject for another book. Meanwhile, let's start with your son or daughter and look at ways we can make the world work for them.

What Can be Done for Our Boys?

History and folklore have given us the map. All we have
to do is follow it. The boy of long ago and the boy of today
need adventure—whether adventure of the mind or
adventure of the body. And many need both. For most boys
it is extremely difficult to spend long periods of time under
other people's direction. They have been horsing around in
school since schools began. They like conflict, whether it's
debating with a teacher or trouncing their best friend on
the sports field. This energy is what psychologist Carl Jung
called animus. While many girls have this same wonderful
competitive energy as well, boys tend to have more animus
than girls. And they have more of it than schools can hold.
As frustrating as it is, boys often don't do very well in high
school because it demands of them a sedentary, stationary
day when what they desire is a day of movement, of action,
and interaction. High schools have not changed appreciably
and yet modern boys, having more access to knowledge of
the outer world, grow more and more restless under the
old system.

For centuries, most people in the US lived in an agrarian
or small-town culture. Boys were raised as their fathers'
helpers and heirs to the family farm or shop. At the turn of
the 19th into the 20th century, 80 percent of all Americans

lived such agrarian or rural environments, away from the big cities. The Second World War saw the beginning of a reversal. As U.S. enterprise and power moved to the cities, the youth of the country moved to where the action was. Soon 20 percent of all Americans lived in agrarian and rural areas and 80 percent lived in cities. The old way of life for boys no longer centered around their fathers; now it centered around their boss. As high technology propelled travel and communications to unheard-of speeds, and unions suffered tone crushing defeat after another, a man's job took over his life. Americans began to work harder and longer. The post-war economy boomed in the 1950s, although not for all and not for long. As inflation hit and rolled into recession in the 60s and 70s, men made more money and worked longer hours, but the money did less. The Women's Movement of the 70s and the flagging economy urged women back into the workforce. Women started competing with men and families, increasingly dependent on two incomes, felt the stress. Men, unused to childcare and household chores, kept the burden on women, forcing women to the "Second Shift"—coming home from work and doing the equivalent of another day's work filled with child care, cooking, laundry, cleaning, homework, etc. Divorce became rampant. Most divorces meant the children spent considerably less time in contact with their fathers. This was a tragedy for children and for fathers. It was a particular tragedy for boys who now were left with less and less male-mentoring.

Often when a tragedy becomes commonplace, it is gradually seen as a norm; but it wasn't a norm for boys. They became restive, rebellious. Many became depressed; many sank into drugs or alcohol. With high technology— games, internet, phones—many drifted into another world. Schools didn't adapt. Boys withdrew.

I admit this is a string of generalizations. But the curious thing about generalizations is that very often they are true. How else do we explain the phenomenal withdrawal of boys from the education system? How do we explain the high rate of second and third generation divorces? And what do we say of the significant number of never-married men in this country? Moreover, with the terrible tragedies of the Vietnam War, and the Afghan and Iraqi wars, the last bastion of male training, the US military, lost much of its reputation, and with this loss a place where young men could learn to be men be among older men became more of a place of economic and educational last resort.

Meanwhile, love seemed to have become rarer. Rape rates, always high in the U.S., started to increase, as boys without mentoring convinced each other that drugging a young woman and raping her was acceptable male fun. The smartphone introduced texting as a dating strategy. Romantic comedies featured hapless, overweight 20-something males actually getting the fabulous girl. But the dream was silly and everyone knew it. "Whatever," became the male teen response to tiresome or harsh realities. "It is what it is," became another. "They're disaffected," yelled countless journal articles. "They're fragile," warned others. That's the bad news.

The good news is that if you know and listen to your kids and guide them through the tough waters, they have a chance of overcoming catastrophe on every level. And if you don't, they won't. Especially with boys, watch to see that their education works for them. If you are a dad, pay special attention to what you do well in the male world and offer it to your kid—whether it's fishing or baseball, budgeting or career. Take your kid with you to places in your world when they are in their early teens. Talk to them about what matters to you. Lead them into the company of other men who can help them, guide them and, perhaps, eventually employ them. If you're the mom, stop fretting and start teaching your son your own skills—if you have a sport, share it. If you have activities that reward you, let them in on that too. Teach your son how women think and what matters to you as a woman and to women in general. When you watch TV or movies together, show them your response to the story or predicaments.

Both parents should make sure your son knows how to cook, do laundry, soothe a baby, create a personal budget, and take care of things once they leave you. Don't be afraid to show him how you organize life, including your finances. If you're a mother with business ability, share that too.

With school, make sure you share what makes sense about it. What is English Lit. for? Didn't it help you become a better writer and to speak about life situations more deeply? Let them know how some or all of it worked positively for you. "Why study Algebra?" they might ask. Explain how it molds the mind to comprehend numbers, logic and the balance of ideas, as well as numbers. If the school is not good for your kid, because of poor teaching or inadequate facilities, look around for others. You are not alone in seeking a good education for your kid. There are so many public alternative schools sprouting up, many of them project-based, giving kids an opportunity to work on studies that integrate writing, history and math, for example, or science research and analysis and art. If these programs are not available, make sure that you guide your young man to resources in your community—art museums, science expos, business fairs—where they can see what is going on in the world and begin to see how they might fit into different worlds.

Don't forget to commend the good in them and in their choices and tell them why, especially in their formative social relationships. "Your friend David seems like a good guy. It seems like he is a good listener," or "Ben is fun to talk to, isn't he?" Approval can speak volumes. It can direct your son in positive directions that will reap positive effects. Approval will also help him relate to people better and lead him to those he can collaborate with, relax with and be egged on to his next step of development.

In all cases, do not give up. Keep educating yourself on how your child learns and what he might need to learn next to advance from an energetic and rewarding childhood into an energetic and rewarding manhood.

What Can Be Done for Our Girls?

It is often good to announce a bias early in a conversation, so regarding the girls, let me reveal my bias right away. I am a strong proponent of girls' high schools and women's colleges. And I am not alone. The Girl Scouts and the Seven Sisters Women's Colleges have consistently produced the vast majority of female leaders in this country in every sphere of our country's life. When girls and young women are together, separated from boys and young men, they gain greater strength, better grades, and achieve more in the larger world than girls consistently raised in a co-educational system. The myth of cat-fighting women destroying each other, so popular in movies, needs to be set aside. The fact is that girls together and out of the sphere of boys often do much better than girls in the social maelstrom of co-education. Educating girls as girls and women as women has had a tremendous fortifying effect on females in all levels of our society. Sincerely consider finding and enrolling your maturing daughter in a girls' high school and look expansively at women's colleges too. Don't think you can afford it? Call the school and find out how hefty their scholarships are. Many gender-specific institutions have healthy endowments. All test scores and satisfaction measurements of girls and teachers show that educating girls and young women separately from boys and young men really boosts girls' achievement levels, and many are much more satisfied without the pressure of male-female socializing happening all day every day, seven days a week.

If an all-girls school is not an option, then be vigilant in your advocacy of your daughter. Watch and listen carefully and if you learn of any sexism in her school, go directly to the source and tell them you will not tolerate it. Schools do not want trouble, and if you become a vocal supporter of your young person and her rights, you will find many allies—parents and often, other educators. Encourage your daughter to take courses that will challenge her. If she has difficulty, do not hesitate to find private tutorial help for her. Many community colleges have lists of student tutors who are young, hip and inexpensive enough for you to get your daughter the support she needs to try some of the "hard stuff." Call the community college career center and ask to interview a few candidates and choose the best one. Stay clear of rabid programs that prepare your kid exclusively for SAT exams. You want your daughter to learn what she needs to learn, not enlist in some lockstep march toward more tests. Teen life is rough enough without activities the will fill her with more worry and less free time to relax and recharge.

Encourage your daughter to socialize with healthy groups or clubs that are fun and which bring her into contact with possible friends in a relaxed way. Is there a good Youth Group in your area attached to the local recreation center or church? Help her get there and back so she doesn't end up in a car full of strangers. Offer to chaperone on trips so that the program can thrive. When you do participate as a chaperone or driver, be sure to stay out of her way while you do this so she doesn't feel spied upon or judged.

Teach her to take care of her body and to enjoy that caring for herself, as women have done for centuries. Spend some quality time with your daughter doing things she likes to do that make her feel lovely and loved. A simple trip to pick up a new t-shirt can be a pleasant and welcome journey for both of you. While you're out with her, offer to buy some of her own toiletries: her own washcloth and towel or favorite soap, new toothbrush or hand cream, and sanitary products. You will be teaching her you care about her and that you want her to enjoy taking care of herself. Showing rather than telling works on so many levels. When you go workout or to simply take a walk, invite her to go with you. Even if she declines, take it with good grace. The lesson is still there: "We women take good care of ourselves physically." Don't forget medical exams. For kids up to 18, you are in charge of making medical appointments, taking her there and paying for her medical care. After 18, teach her how to make her yearly check-up appointment and when she goes, offer to go with her the first time or at least accompany her to the office. If sex is in the offing, help her choose proper birth control. Don't leave her pregnancy and disease protection to the high school sex education class.

What is she reading, thinking, viewing? Dip into her influences—after she has gone to a movie with her friends and tells you she liked it, make the effort to go to it yourself and then talk about it with a deep respect for her observations and responses to it. If she liked it and you didn't, listen to what she says about it and then give the same kind of critique you would share with a beloved friend: "I can see what you mean about the acting. It was excellent, as you say. I did think it was a bit too long." In all cases, make your time with your daughter about her interests, not about yours. That's what your friends are for.

Because mother/daughter stuff can get hectic, don't forget to ask your friends to act as doulas to midwife her move into adulthood and away from you. In all cases, teach her by word and example how to date and how to fall in love. For both moms and dads and any other loving adult members of your household, make sure your beloved young woman feels respected and protected. Set the parameters around her clearly so she is well-treated. Young men or women who come to pick her up should come to the front door. No honking in the street for your kid. If this happens, it is not only appropriate but mandatory that either you or your partner go out to the honking young person and explain: "Hi, I think you're here to pick up our daughter. We have a rule that all people who come to pick her up come to the front door, ring the bell and come in to meet us. So, come on in and visit with us before you two go out." Smile, and welcome your visitor into your home.

If she is going any distance outside of your house for an evening, make sure that your teen girl has plenty of money in her purse so that she can phone for a cab, wherever she is. Give her $100 or so, and perhaps have a credit card with a simple allowable balance and make sure she understands these represent a loan for emergencies. If she finds herself in a bad part of town with a bad date, or her car breaks down, she can always call a cab or AAA and get the heck outta there.

Let Us Be There For All Teens

In every case and situation, make sure your young person is well-fed and well-watered. Keep delicious and nutritious food in the house. From the time they are youngsters, help them learn what foods give them energy, what foods can help them relax and ease tension. Check out what is being served in the school cafeteria and from the school vending machines and start a letter-writing campaign if healthy improvement is necessary.

See that your young people—female and male—are well-rested by watching their daily rhythms and helping them get in sync with them. Everyone knows that teens are growing and therefore need much more sleep than most adults. Many schools are now starting the school day later out of respect for this. See if you can form a movement in this direction by speaking up at PTA meetings or by gathering like-minded adults to approach the principal and the district superintendent. Engage your child in this kind of activism as well. This can be good practice for creating productive change. Children created the movement to end smoking in public spaces. Ending junk food in the school cafeteria or extending sleep time for high school students may be the next movement your daughter or son can create for themselves and the generations after them.

What Should Education Be?

Education should be many things to many people. It should be the focus of our national efforts. It should be broad enough to serve the classic intellectual as well as the gifted mechanic. It should be energetic enough to encourage innovation while preserving a realistic sense of the past including its accomplishments, disasters, and achievements. Education should be full of excitement. That's what it should be. So when you look at a school, here's what you're looking for: the place should have an air of energy and purpose. In a good school, the rooms will be quiet with the intensity of real work. Kids will be intent on working, listening, or talking and it will sound like something important is going on. There will be a positive feeling of getting things done. Here's what it should not be: it should not be a playpen for spoiled brats set on disrupting learning with a quest for a continuous stream of stimuli. You know a good school when you find it, because people are involved and working or moving with purpose. And although no high school can be silent, the school which has something to offer the growing mind, body, and spirit is relatively serene. People are working at something they care about. They are engrossed in rewarding effort. They are doing something that has meaning, that they respect and that is built on the concept of respect for them and their skills.

Education is meant to make every person into their own teacher, as Thomas Paine said. The gift of schooling is that the resources and the social life for a teenager are in one place. The curriculum must give an idea of how all aspects of the world work; which means it should offer a study of the natural world, as well as the people-made one. And it should honor both. It should examine basic concepts of how physical, economic, social, and political systems work, and should encourage a consideration of differences where there are some, and complementarities where there are some. It should never limit discussion of the current situation and its implications. In many schools, the decision to connect the classroom with the outside world had had powerful positive results.

Next Steps

Time is running short and my editor is waiting; so, in my classic directive style, let me say that there is a lot we can do for our kids in school. Here is a draft list that I think each of us can start to move on, solo or in groups:

Elevating Teaching: Teaching used to be a "calling," a spiritual command to do good. Let us make educating our young a great and honorable profession again. Taking a page from great education systems such as that of Finland, let us seek out the finest minds, the most creative intellects, and train them to become a kind of elite, like doctors and lawyers. Let us pay them as well as we pay our doctors and our lawyers. Then step back and watch kids blossom.

Designing Approaches that Satisfy the Needs of Boys and Girls: Let us look upon gender learning differences as exciting challenges instead of annoying burdens. Let us create opportunities for girls to blossom and for boys to grow as well. Whether we create gender-specific classes or design student-driven, project-based learning, or both, let us give more respect for the different ways boys and girls learn.

Making Use of Community Expertise: Let us create special certificates for leaders in business, science and technology, arts, design, human services, psychology, law, politics, banking, computers, media, non-profit development, writing, and other great paths to become visiting experts in our schools. The successful in so many fields can share their genius in their crafts and in their networks so our students will be groomed in knowledge and connections that can lead them to meaningful work.

Cutting Back on Standardized Testing: Let us end standardized testing, or use it only every second or third year of school, and let us limit the testing to one week and one week only in the school year. Let us bring back essay exams and explore more useful ways of measurement, like the Johnson O'Connor tests, that discover innate abilities that our young people can revel in and follow into meaningful occupations.

Beefing Up Paid Internship Opportunities: Let us also train a cadre of new guidance counselors and parents who can shape course choices and who can introduce students to internships that will give them real-life training. In this way schools and parents in collaboration can help our young people explore different fields and opportunities, and students can see what work they are best suited for and can choose advanced training or education that will suit them for these desired paths.

Bringing Back Art, Music, Theater, Dance, and Playtime: Studies have consistently shown over decades of research that students who have arts and play activities as an integral part of their school lives consistently do better in all kinds of thinking, including "hard sciences" and mathematics. Studies also show these programs encourage creativity and team work so essential in their later adult lives. So let's take two steps back and revive these lost courses of study and watch our kids expand in them.

Redesigning the Community College System for Better Results: With budget cuts, many students cannot easily get into the courses they need for an AA within two years. They languish in the system often for years. Let us make sure the requisite courses are available to them. At the same time, let us persuade quality colleges to accept students who have a proven 2-year success record in community college, even if they have not completed a two-year associates' degree. Let us try both strands and see if both methods work, or if one is more successful than another.

There are countless other ways that we can help our young to both rewarding and useful educational experiences. Let us keep thinking, doing, and improving the education of our young people. They deserve it, most certainly. And our future depends upon it.

In the meantime, for our boys and for our girls, make it a priority to be sure your kid is in a decent school. This is critical. Your young person should not be in a school that has a high number of dropouts. They should not be somewhere that is violent. If your local school is merely mediocre—not well-ranked on state scores, with limited course choices or a bad rep among teens themselves– consider whether you can make real efforts in the school to make real improvements. While your kid is still in middle school, visit the principal and find out what plans and funding are available to change the school from mediocre to great. If that visit proves the situation is hopeless, consider moving to where your kid will be better educated. Many, many parents are doing this, renting out their houses or leaving their beloved apartment to a different, often smaller, venue for the sake of their kids' futures.

Or consider shifting your kid to a better district without moving. Many school districts will allow transfers. Call the district you are considering and find out. Offer to become the volunteer of the year, if they take your kid. If that doesn't look possible, then seriously consider private school. Cannot afford it? Look to scholarship help and help from grandparents or relatives who want to see your kid thrive. Don't leave this important step toward your kid's happiness to chance.

Chapter 11—Success

To most people in Western culture, success is what a friend of mine once called "the spouse, the car, the kids, the house with the white picket fence." But in many places of the world and even in many parts of the privileged West, success would be one decent meal a day. In other parts of the world, success might be the ability to meditate for an hour or the ability to bring a ferry into port on time day after day. Success might, in some places and times, be the essential acknowledgment that one is content with oneself and one's place in the world.

In the United States particularly, success is a very serious subject, though what it is dressed in often looks like fun. In the U.S. success is money and lots of things to buy with it. The "rules of success" are touted constantly from the Internet, television programs, advertising, on the radio in songs, and of course, in movies. Rarely do we see any commercial displays depicting a family living in a two-bedroom house with a leaky toilet and a dog that is dying of old age. All successful people have gone to Harvard or Yale. All vacations are two weeks at the best resorts. People have nice teeth, clean sweatshirts, new cars. It looks like a total state of freedom. All a kid has to do is stay in school, get good grades and/or come up with a dynamite high-tech product or musical invention and they're solid. Yet, at most schools, children are pummeled with exams, homework assignments and busy work designed to grade them, judge them and stamp them as ready for the office cubicle in the nearest corporation. Then they can step out into the world of buying things and having things. This is not a plan for a free, engaged citizenry; this is training for sheep. So kids are confused. What is success and how do you get there, really?

The answer is simple. Success is happiness. And it is true that happiness often includes work. Work that is difficult. Work that is sometimes boring. Work that is challenging. Often, work that doesn't pay well. But success/happiness can be obtained with a strategy. And strategy begins with a dream.

Every person has had a dream or a vision of who they wanted be and what they wanted to be doing. This dream comes in a sleeping or waking state, usually as a whole image but sometimes in parts over days and often when the person is very young—by young I mean 3 or 4 years old. Ask anyone you know when they knew what they wanted to be when they grew up, and they will tell you a story rich in detail. A friend of mine became a quilter. Her dream of her future happened when she was 4. Her dad was a fabric salesman to tailors. Every night, he came home from his work with a huge ring of fabric samples. He would drop the ring at the living room door and hurry into the kitchen to greet his wife. My friend would drag the ring of cloths into the living room, unclasp it, and begin laying the fabrics out on the floor. First in fans of color, later in patterns. She made her designs huge enough to cover the whole floor and loved every one of them. Today she makes her own fabric designs, instilled by the memory of her playtime with her father's ring of samples.

You know of stories like this one. A tiny child who flew down the road joyfully on a bike and today as an adult organizes bike trips around the country. The kid who blew up things in the backyard and today is an engineer specializing in demolition for transportation projects. Doctors are made watching over a favorite grandparent in a hospital. Lawyers are made winning arguments at the dinner table. The thrill of early success is potent.

Fostering Success

By watching closely what intrigues your young person, you will see interests arise. These interests are your kid's key to the future. Nourish these interests—not because they will lead to fame and fortune necessarily, but because they are paths to self-knowledge, self-growth, self-expression, and self-expansion in the world. They may be athletic interests—roller hockey or soccer, baseball or ballet. They may revolve around one of the arts—writing, painting, sculpture/ceramics or explorations in multi-media and other realms of expression. They may be musical—anything from the didgeridoo to the violin. Or their interest may be a study that integrates a combination of many aspects of themselves, such as theater or film or other performance realms. Sign them up, get them there on time, cheer them on, and admire what they are doing—whether they are the leader or supporting player. Respect what they are exploring, even if it differs from what you know, think, or believe.

Politics became and still is a focus in our house, although we had differing opinions about issues, and about how to take action in support of our beliefs. I found that letting my children explore their own avenues gave them many important lessons and enabled them to become their own people—people who were learned and comfortable in themselves and what they believed, and knew how to express these beliefs in the world. With your own children, check in with what they are doing and how safely they are doing it, and you will often feel much relieved. In one such check-in about my son's political activism, Max said reassuringly, "Don't worry Mom, I have no interest in being arrested."

Your young person's interests may be spiritual. They may become more ardent in the family faith. They may want to go to religious services more often. Be with them. They may want to visit other religious centers. Go with them. Perhaps your young person wants to salute their intellectual side with greater intensity than they are getting at school. Take them to lectures that interest them or movies that may interest them. Purchase or borrow books or materials that they are longing for. When Max mentioned he wanted to know more about how the universe works, I kept my eyes open for something that might encourage his curiosity. Soon after he spoke to me, I noticed a paperback by the physicist Isaac Asimov at a garage sale. It cost a dime. I put the book at the end of Max's bed one afternoon while he was out and when he came home, he began reading it immediately. Science grew into a lifelong passion for Max, and today he is in engineering school and already has a job that revolves around science. The little book may not have led much further than a few rainy afternoons of reading, but wasn't it still worth my time and interest in his satisfaction to encourage his enjoyment and knowledge?

When Gina found clay was her medium in freshman year of high school, she told me sadly that there were no more advanced classes at the school for her. I did the research and discovered one of the country's best-known clay sculptors had a studio within walking distance of Gina's high school. I signed her up for a very modestly priced series of lessons. Today Gina is a sculptor, photographer, and teacher, who loves the connection to clay she found when she was 14.

In all cases, when you see an interest, try to actively nurture it, with no thought of it becoming a career. And no pressure. Here again is a Gina story that taught me so much as her mother. From a very young age, Gina had amazing aquatic skills. She could swim very well and really excelled at diving. The people at the pool where we swam used to gather in large crowds to watch her. Eventually the attention she garnered took away her happiness in the sport. Her father and I were willing to go elsewhere, find her a coach, and really nurture her talent. We consulted with swim coaches and introduced her to trainers. But the thrill was gone for Gina. She went on to her passion for art and today is very satisfied with the support she received for this, her deeper interest. So, if any one of your daughter's or son's passions proves to be a passing fancy or short-term learning romance, let it go. Other appealing activities will appear that will eventually lead to long-term satisfactions. Try to keep your expenditures reasonable so that if an interest dwindles, you will not be blaming your daughter or son for wasting a lot of your money. Borrow or rent equipment or instruments. Register your young person for continuing-education courses before you cart them to a master class at the university. Schedule them for an hour-long tutorial with an expert in the field of interest before you spend serious money on the summer-long intensive trip in a distant state or land.

In all cases, enjoy watching their exploration. The mind, the body, and the spirit are advancing on paths of their own. And that's a good thing. And don't forget that their school has courses and resources that you may help them explore. Gently encourage them to register for classes they might enjoy outside of the realm of the ordinary. Many kids are afraid that this exploration may not end well, and will show up as a dark mark on their records. Clubs might be the answer in this case. A student can look into something new that looks good on their record and may lead to a brave dive into a new area of learning, when they are ready. And it is way easier logistically for them to find their fulfillment at their school if the school has the resources, the educators, and counselors who can help. As we have noted, some do, some don't. It's important that you know as much as you can about your young person's high school and what is going on there.

Cultivating Dreams

Do you want to cultivate your kid's success? Of course you do! Then gently, respectfully, find out what their first dream looked like and felt like, and work from there. Be careful not to press too specifically on the dream. My friend with her love of fabric design might have become an architect or a creator of jigsaw puzzles. Some dreams take many varied steps. Be aware that the teen years are very complex and demanding and, in many cases, frightening. So if there seems to be a stumble on the dream, especially in the first year or two of college, step in and help. One teen I know wanted with all his heart to become a video game designer. He talked about it every time I saw him. When he got to college, he shifted the dream to something he didn't want and really doesn't like. When I asked him what happened to the original dream, he told me, "I couldn't hack the math." His parents, not watching over him during his crucial first year of college, didn't notice that the simple expense of a tutor or the gentle guidance to the student services center, where a tutor was free, might have kept this young man's dream alive. Instead of lending the magic combo of some information and support, they let him "find his way." One parent might have said, "I understand that you are not doing well in math and that this might hold you back from your dream. I had a similar problem when I got to college. Can I tell you what worked for me?" Then the parent could have worked with the kid—giving them support and information and made the wayward dream a possibility. Instead, today this perfectly wonderful and viable vision of a life of fun and rewarding work is now sitting somewhere in the back of this young man's psyche, pretty much gone. It might surface years from now, but wouldn't it be better and more efficient if the kid was helped to do it now? So do watch, look, encourage, your kid's dreams. Be open-minded, especially when looking over school curricula and course choices particularly in high school. Don't discourage courses you think "will not get them anywhere." And here's why:

Many American schools over-emphasize math and science, thinking that technology is the only path to the future. Yet studies consistently show that art—painting, photography, sculpture, drama, music, creative writing— serve to boost not only the highly touted test scores, but all aspects of a young person's development in all kinds of areas and disciplines. This means that if you want to see your kid excel in computer sciences, it might be wise to encourage those imaginative studies, like the arts and courses that encourage a broader world view and personal knowledge, such as history, literature and psychology. A more- balanced education helps assure that you two will be able to relate better into the future, too.

Be sure your kid feels that what they are doing and where they are going is worthwhile, that you respect them and can see them succeeding. All young people need to know two things before they leave high school: that they have skills the world needs, and that the world is eager to greet them with opportunity. Yet year after year, at graduation time, newspapers bemoan the lack of jobs, of good positions in good schools, of promise available to this new group of graduates. This is poppycock. And dangerous poppycock, too. It is language designed to make frightened workers who will take any job, no matter how dismal, and accept any kind of pay, no matter how low it is.

We become what we think about. And if we are going to tell young people there is no place for them unless they bend their skills and their wills to capricious economic forecasts, then we will end up with cynical, unfulfilled adults ill-prepared to participate in the work of family and community.

SECTION 3: BEYOND NUTS AND BOLTS

Chapter 12—
Redefining Success

Success begins with a path. A vision that points in a direction. The path is not easily found. It takes a willingness to find it, and then it takes another kind of willingness to devote oneself to it. I was watching a television talk show several years ago that revolved around four young men, each of whom had become a millionaire before he was 30. Now this is a kind of success anyone can admire. But of course, not many can do such a thing. I listened to the show with only one ear as I washed dishes and shook out the table cloth preparing to set the table for dinner. I expected each one to worship materialism and talk about numbers and three out of the four did just that. Each of the first three young men said something that described little of his journey. Either they were shy, they didn't want to share the secrets of their success, or they were just boring, I could not tell. Finally we came to the fourth young man. He was dressed like the others—good suit, gleaming white shirt, decent tie. But he didn't look like the others. His energy was wonderfully intense. He fairly jumped out of the television screen. And yet he was thoughtful. Clearly, he had deliberated upon this question more than once before. And so he was ready.

"The first thing you must do is form a vision of what success would be to you," he said distinctly. Then he paused to give emphasis to his next sentence. "Then you must surround yourself only with people who want to see you make it." He paused. "And get rid of everyone else in your life who says you can't."

The audience sat stunned. And then, as the host announced a commercial break, they broke into applause. The young man's statement was so vivid, so honest, so thrilling, so true. We, none of us, need to be hounded by the naysayers in life. They are there naturally and always will be. But we don't need negativity fed to us as a daily diet. It will only lead us to self-doubt and changeability and sadness. To have a plan is a fine thing. To alter that plan from time, in order to hone it, is fine too. But to do anything in this world, we need support and no one needs support to go forth and conquer more than teenagers. They need financial support, and emotional support, and sometimes physical support. How we give all these support elements in the right amounts is one of the toughest roads to being a parent. We want them to leave us, but we also want to be there for them. We want them attached to our lives as part of a continuing family, but we want to be sure the string is long enough for them to get away. We also want them to be able to come back with freedom, without tripping over our lives, without strangling in our methods and our pasts.

Success can come to a person quickly or it can take many years to achieve. And then it might take a different direction. Success is not a static thing. To be human is to experience and generate change. The nature of human life is that it is varied. Triumphs and easy wins, satisfaction, rest, peace, comfort, connectedness, extravagance, love, laughter, joy, all coming in different amounts at different times. The nature of human life is also loss, failure, disappointment, anger, frustration, poverty, loneliness, pain. At any time we can feel successful just by understanding and accepting this. One school of modern psychology claims that we should try to steer clear of surging highs and crashing lows and seek an even space in all of our life's activities. Others propose a life of adventure and constant seeking. We cannot say what success will look like to all people or even to one other person, like our child. If success is happiness, we do not ever know how long it should last. We can say that it is both a creation and an attitude. I have often worked with young people from poor neighborhoods who must work three jobs to support their families and who also go to school. Yet with all the demands upon them, they have a feeling of living rich lives, of creating strong supportive family and friendship bonds, and they say they are happy in their lives. I know many children from rich families who have few responsibilities who cannot say as much.

You can help your child achieve success by helping them envision what they are trying to accomplish and how they would like to get there. Twice a year I review my life. I take a piece of 8 1/2 by 11 inch paper and fold it in half and then fold it in six columns. I label the columns financial, physical, relationship, spiritual, emotional, rest/relaxation. Then I fill out the top part of the chart detailing how well I have done in the last year—all my accomplishments in each area. Then I do the bottom part of the chart detailing what I want to accomplish in the year ahead. I show it to my children. Often, I tack it to the fridge so everyone can look at it whenever they like. I encourage my children to do the same and I help them make a plan from the chart that will enable them to reach their goals. Toward the end of the year, we look again at our charts and see how close we have come to creating the kind of success that matters to each of us. There is no judgment; just positive energy. I do not try to sway my children from their goals, although I sometimes help them organize them so they are in easy-to-do steps.

Again, it bears repeating: remember that life, especially young life, is changeable. It is important to let young people, aware that the country may be in crisis or contributing to crises elsewhere, explore, critique, challenge and imagine alternative paths and how they might contribute to improving the world. Teenagers are natural dissidents. You once were one, too. And perhaps you are still. So you know that dissent is a device for edging away from home, for establishing independence, for making one's own world and entering into it with a sense of promise and of freedom. Confess it. This is what you want for your child. Prizes and awards and degrees are nice but the essence of life here is both bigger and smaller than that.

On a more practical level, as well, it is best not to become too agitated about plans your young person is making. My son wanted to buy a motorcycle. It filled me with private worry, but he was 18 and he has a right to live his own life at some point. I did not tell him much about my worries, but did look into insurance for him, and from time to time I would mention a bike I had seen for sale.

Eventually, he decided he did not want a motorcycle. He wanted to save money and travel a variety of different ways on his year between high school and college. I could have started an anxious tirade when he first mentioned the motorcycle idea. Or I could have waited and watched and helped him research what he needed, and see what became of his decision. His change in plans is not so much a failure as a re-assessment. I am sure any trip he takes in his life will be meaningful and full of adventures—both benign and sometimes, even hair-raising. But each trip will be his trip. Because it will be his creation, marked by his own assessments and learning, it will have both meaning and value for him. It will make him happy. And that is what I call success.

Chapter 13—Spirituality, Creativity and Idealism

The teen mind is a growing mind. Science tells us that at few other times in our lives will our brain expand so much and so fast. Hormones surge—the body grows, sexuality comes into a new stage ready for procreation, and ideas come as rapidly as rain falling from a spreading sky.

Here is a time of great creativity. Here, too is a time of wonder. Your teen sees things, knows things, and senses things in a great new way. They are full of vigor and promise. And then they bump up against the terrible realities of the world.

When my daughter was three, we were driving through the streets of downtown Philadelphia on a snowy Sunday morning in February. The day was bright, yet the freezing cold air was sharp as a knife bite. As we drove we saw homeless people struggling against the bitter wind, walking to a doorway for cover.

"Oh! What are those people doing?" she called out from the back seat.

"They are homeless, they have nowhere to live, and they are trying to get out of the cold," Gina's father said.

"Oh," she said and her little face frowned as she sadly stared out the window at the poor.

A few minutes later we passed a construction site with scaffolding pressed against structures waiting for Monday and a new day of work.

"What is that?" Gina called out pointing at the new walls around hollow, unfinished shells.

"Those are new houses," Gina's dad replied. "They are not finished yet."

"Oh, good," said Gina with a happy sigh. "Soon those poor people will have some place to live!"

The baby Gina grew up into the young woman Gina who knew those houses were never going to go to the poor. And it made her very angry. It aroused her to serious and concerted action. She stirred many consciences. She fought many battles and is fighting them to this day. At the age of 16 she began to work to end poverty through action and through art.

We never told the baby Gina that she was wrong about the houses going up in Philadelphia. She learned in her own time. And we never told her when she was a teenager that she was fighting a useless fight. Because as far as we were concerned, her youthful struggle to save the world was a useful call to us to redouble our lost efforts to do right in a troubled society.

And this is what the growing mind, the growing body, and the growing spirit do. They gear up the person to reach new stages and expand their capabilities and insights in many new ways: physical, intellectual, social, emotional, psychological, and spiritual. It is one of the greatest gifts, if not THE greatest gift, that young people have to give our society. Their purity of mind and heart is not to be trifled with. It is a gift from beyond us. We should treasure it and pay attention.

So, do not be surprised if your young person sees a wrong and sets out to right it. Stand back, please, while they are making their placards and striding off to the state capitol or to Washington. Instead, lend an ear and learn about something new, some cause worth your attention as well as theirs. Because it is only in supporting the calls of youth urging us to step away from our worries over mortgages and car payments and taxes that we can all change the world for the better. It is the only sure way we know. Only by using the energy and idealism of youth can we make our old world new again. It is the job of youth to recall us to service for good. And it is our job to follow them.

At the same time, the sister elements of this growing psyche are creativity and spirituality. You may find your young person leaving drawings of formulas or ellipses or calculations on the floor around their bed. They may be designing new clothes or sewing new things or drawing and painting constantly. They may be listening to a lot of music or joining a band. They may become immersed in the drama club, or dance classes. They may take things apart. And forget to put them back together again. They may leave their precious objects strewn everywhere about their rooms. Don't touch! Unless it looks like it will catch the room on fire, leave well enough alone.

Imagine there is a sign constantly on their door saying: "Go away. I am magical and I am making the world new!"

Just the same, the rise of spirituality, stemming from the same growing psyche, may make your eyes widen. Parents, whose little children loved familiar religious instruction and said their prayers before bed, find their teen suddenly reading deeply in foreign forms of worship. They may quote Zoroaster, the Dalai Lama, the tales of the great Goddesses of a distant past. This is normal. Parents who have professed no faith for years may find their young person eager to go to church or temple—curious to look deep into a world they may have set aside. This too is normal. And a wake-up call for you.

Where is your idealism? Where is your creativity? Where is your spiritual life? Carl Jung once said, "In adulthood, we seek the spiritual life of our youth." Are you perhaps longing for a distant time and place where you prayed every day, where you had a dear and tender or strong and vital faith? Can you not go back to one of those precious places that once watered your soul and drink again?

In dealing with your young person, be very careful with this, one of your child's most important growth spurts. Give space, with, of course, a careful eye that notices signs of alienation or drug use. Participation and help are the greatest safeguards. If political activism is the growing desire, enter into the fray. Do go with your young person to marches or meetings that matter to them. Offer to drive them to these events. Introduce them to people you know who are making a difference in the world and who have turned youthful activist ardor into an adult career and practice.

Do find imaginative outlets for creative energies. Pay for the extra dance class or music or art experiences they need. Point them in the direction of inexpensive events that even they can afford. Gallery openings are often eye-opening and they are certainly inexpensive. Turn your young person on to special student rates at museums and performances. Youth is full of first tries, so expect that many of these endeavors may not pan out. Instead of spending money on buying fancy supplies, outfits, tools or instruments, rent them, scour the thrift shops or check for used bargains online. If the interest takes off, support it. Start small and watch and see if your kid really is suited to this or that interest. Don't be petulant if your young person takes only one year of judo and then switches to mountain biking. By spending modest amounts here and there, you will eventually find things that fit and that make your young person feel settled into something important. Then invest in that interest and help them to do their share too, so that they can make this interest into a passion and from a passion perhaps into a life.

As for spirituality, your practice is the best exemplar. Ask your teen how they feel about integrating into your practice and you integrating into theirs. Can you meet somewhere on a plane where each of you respects and shares the other's spiritual endeavors? One usher in my church has two teenage boys. They never come to church except on the Sundays he ushers. On those Sundays he persuades the boys to be there by asking them to help. It isn't often, a few times a year. But the boys feel included and it may bring them back more and more in later years. Who knows?

In our family, we had a marriage of many faiths. So it was both necessity and desire that caused us to create our own rituals at home. Grace at the table is key to our days when we are together. We use one that came a long time ago from Gina's nursery school. We hold hands and say solemnly: "It is nice to sit down and have dinner with your family. Amen." Even our littlest new member now clamors for grace before each family meal.

We often light a candle in the morning to greet the day. We mark special events like birthdays, the school year's end, as well as holidays, with readings from a favorite poem or a passage from a beloved book. Sometimes we sing. We have found that even "Row, row, row your boat" can be sacred music if we approach it that way. Sometimes we sit quietly and breathe before we begin a task or chore. The washing of dishes, the greeting of guests for a party, the leaving on a long trip, all can be sacred occasions. All can become places where we teach our beloved children how much we love our family and love them in it.

We began noticing and celebrating all of these precious moments because we were a family and because our children insisted on it: "Let's do something special!" they would say. Today they both are idealists, artists, knowledgeable and spiritual people. And I have discovered that I am, too.

Recommended Reading List

As parents we get sustenance from many sources. Here is part of the reading list that helped me help my own kids and the many others I have served:

Books:

Dreikurs, Rudolf, *Children the Challenge*

Edelman, Marion Wright, *The Measure of Our Success*

Evatt, Cris, *He/She: 60 Significant Differences Between Men & Women*

Heidegger, Martin, *Poetry, Language, Thought*

Hanh, Tich Nhat, *Peace is Every Step*

Hillman, James and Ventura, Michael, *We've Had a Hundred Years of Therapy and We're Getting Worse*

Hilton, Joni, *Five Minute Miracles*

Heschel, Abraham Joshua, *The Sabbath*

Keats, John, "Lamia" in *The Collected Works of John Keats*

Leach, Penelope, *Children First*

Levinson, Daniel, *Seasons of a Man's Life*

Llewelyn, Grace, *Teenage Liberation Handbook*

Louv, Richard, *Last Child in the Woods*

Mander, Jerry, *Four Arguments for the Elimination of Television*

Mander, Jerry, *In the Absence of the Sacred*

McKnight-Trontz, *The Good Citizens Handbook- A Guide to Proper Behavior*

Miller, Alice, *Drama of the Gifted Child*

Miller, Alice, *For Your Own Good*

Newman, Katherine, *No Shame in My Game*

Satir, Virginia, *Peoplemaking*

Sanders, Barry, *A is for Ox: The Collapse of Literacy & the Rise of Violence in an Electronic Age*

Shah, Idries, *The Wisdom of the Idiots*

Steiner, George, *Real Presences*

Taylor, Jeremy, *Dream Work*

Winsatt, William Upski. *No More Prisons*

Reports:
American Council on Education, *Minorities in Education 2008, Status Report*

Bureau of Labor Statistics, *Reports on Education, 2011-2013*

Symonds, Bill, *Harvard University Paths to Prosperity Report, February 2011*

Kotkin, Joel *Newsweek, Are Millenials the Screwed Generation? July 16, 2012*
Presidents' Council of Economic Advisors, *Annual Report, 2011*

About the Author

Mary Ann Maggiore is a coach, consultant, educator and public speaker who shares her insights through workshops, seminars, presentations and private consultations. She has thrilled both national and international audiences with her enthusiastic approach to the challenges of parenting teens. The President of the United States, the California Senate and the California State Assembly have commended her innovative programs and methods. Mary Ann is also the first recipient of the Working Solutions Community Impact Award. Her work has been lauded by the media, including NPR and the Los Angeles Times. Mary Ann has a BA from Swarthmore College as well as a Masters of Divinity from Starr King School of Ministry and has served as a Chaplain at Marin General Hospital counseling patients and their families. Mary Ann is president of Five 4 Five which guides young people to successful adulthoods.

She is also the happy mother of two teens who became sane and successful adults. To learn more about Mary Ann, contact her at: maryannmaggiore@gmail.com

36464419R00100

Made in the USA
Charleston, SC
04 December 2014